SALADLOVE

David Bez of Salad Pride

SALADLOVE

260 Crunchy, savory, and filling meals you
can make every day

appetite
by RANDOM HOUSE

To my mom.
To my family.

Text copyright © 2014 by David Bez
Design and layout © 2014 Quadrille Publishing
Limited

Publishing Director: Jane O'Shea
Creative Director: Helen Lewis
Senior Editor: Céline Hughes
Designer and Photographer: David Bez
Production: Vincent Smith, Aysun Hughes,
Leonie Kellman, Sasha Hawkes

Originally published in the United Kingdom by
Quadrille Publishing Ltd., London, in 2014.

All photographs except photo on page 30
copyright © 2014 by David Bez.
Photograph on page 30 copyright © 2014 by
Michelle Turriani

Published in Canada by Appetite by Random
House®, a division of Random House of Canada
Limited, a Penguin Random House Company

Appetite by Random House® and colophon are
registered trademarks of Random House of Canada
Limited

Library and Archives of Canada Cataloguing in
Publication is available upon request

ISBN: 978-0-449-01676-3
eBook ISBN: 978-0-449-01677-0

Cover design by La Tricia Watford
Cover photography by David Bez
Printed and bound in China

www.randomhouse.ca

10 9 8 7 6 5 4 3 2

appetite
by RANDOM HOUSE

Penguin
Random
House

CONTENTS

INTRODUCTION

THIS IS NOT A COOKBOOK

I'm not a chef; I'm a designer and food lover raised in Milan. This is a book about why I love salads, what inspired me to make a new one every day, and how you can do the same. It won't teach you how to cook—it is a collection of salad combinations that I've actually prepared and eaten. I'm not a food stylist or a food photographer, but I made these plates of salad for my lunch and photographed them before tucking in. They were made at my desk in my office, when I have just an hour (sometimes half) to get my lunch and eat it, like most people. Sure, there are a lot of things you can buy at restaurants (too expensive), or from the grocery store or supermarket (not as fresh as I would like). I wanted something healthy, fresh, tasty, and quick and often that's difficult to find. I like good food and I'm quite fussy about it. I know I'm not alone. For most nine-to-fivers, lunch is a functional moment in the day, merely a way to replenish—rarely a pleasure. I do not see it that way: my Italian genes scream loudly and refuse to surrender to eating any old thing.

Moreover, I don't trust how stores and supermarkets select and process their so-called "healthy" foods. I care about where my ingredients have been sourced and how they have been put together. I don't want them to contain weird chemicals with crazy scientific names. I want to be able to choose something that is truly healthy, not "healthier" or even worse, fake "healthy" like some low-fat but sugar-loaded yogurts or cereals.

I've been reading a lot about nutrition, eating seasonally, the properties of various ingredients, vegetarianism, veganism, raw veganism, blood pH levels, local farming, organic farming, and so on. As a result, I feel more knowledgeable on many food-related issues (although sometimes I feel more confused than ever—is soy milk good for you or not?!). The basic principle that most people seem to agree on is that we need to eat a lot of grains and fresh fruits and vegetables not just because it's better for us, but because it's better for the planet as well. It's as simple as that!

I have another simple lunch rule: I want to finish my lunch feeling energized and ready to work. If I feel tired and sleepy, that is not a good meal. On top of that, I always try to buy organic, fair trade, sustainable, and locally sourced food as much as I can. Why? I'm a dad, I care about the future of my son, and, yes, I know it sounds grandiose, but together, simply by changing our dietary habits, we can all make an impact, and our choices can give us a better world.

1,000 DAYS OF OFFICE LUNCHES, OR MORE

In order to be able to eat the healthy, fresh food I wanted, I decided to prepare my own lunch every day in the office. I wanted these meals to be something easy enough to prepare at my desk. Mind you, there aren't that many things you can prepare at your desk, especially if you hate the microwave. Yes, I hate the microwave. I have never liked the idea of warming up preprepared food in a plastic box. While I love to cook at home, cooking in the office is not practical, so I had to compromise. Some ingredients—the fresh ones—could be brought to the office and refrigerated; others could be prepared in the office with a kettle (or even a hot water dispenser); and others could be brought in precooked (such as last night's dinner leftovers).

I started by doing a weekly shop on Monday morning, buying enough ingredients for the week ahead, plus a little more, just in case. I always looked at what was in season and, depending on my mood, I relied on a mixture of improvisation and planning. And the food that was left over on Friday afternoons I brought home. I kept my fresh ingredients in the communal refrigerator, taking up a whole shelf (my colleagues probably hate me as a result). I transformed my desk drawer into a kitchen storage area, keeping essential tools there such as a cutting board, a proper knife, a small salad spinner, a can opener, and some dried ingredients, including spices, canned beans, nuts, and dried fruits (some of which I also snacked on during the day).

And every day at lunchtime I turned my desk into a little kitchen countertop, creating temporary havoc—chaotic but controlled. That is, until I started cutting raw beet and got my hands all "bloody" just before a big meeting. Now I wear latex gloves when I'm dealing with that sort of dangerous stuff.

I find myself relaxing quite a lot while I chop and mix, shuck and rinse. My lunch break has become a little Zen moment. It's not just a matter of preparing and eating, it's the pleasure of smelling and feeling the ingredients and flavors of the food. There is an interesting mindfulness when you allow yourself to be silent and concentrate on the task at hand. You can also free up your senses, even for just 15 minutes. Preparing food is a very rich sensory experience. There are not just colors and shapes to exploit, but new experiments using unscripted combinations of texture, taste, aroma, and visual appeal. I use my imagination to make each lunch break an exciting exploration of as-yet-unexplored food terrains.

As soon as I began making these balanced, nutritious salads, my colleagues were immediately attracted to the idea and kept wanting to tuck into my creations. "What are you preparing there?" they would constantly ask. "What a great smell of basil!" they exclaimed. Everyone was fascinated by my culinary flights of salad fancy. So it occurred to me that they might be of interest to a wider audience, and I started to take pictures and post them on a blog. It has now been three years since I began creating a new and different lunch every day. Really! Three years! I can't believe the number of combinations I've created—some extremely delicious, some really good, others . . . I've learned a lot along the way and I've definitely honed my skills. It took three years to find the magic formula. Most of all, I wanted to demonstrate that I could make a healthy lunch at my desk but, just as important, I wanted what I was eating to be a yummy, sophisticated, and complete meal. I believe I have succeeded, but it's up to you to decide.

When I first embarked on the project, I didn't know how to begin. For one thing, I wasn't on a diet. I didn't need to lose weight; I just wanted to eat right and I still wanted plenty of flavors in my meal. So I started with some random tests and quickly realized that what I was doing was making salads. How did I define a salad? Given my office constraints, my lunch had to be a cold dish, made from various cold ingredients, mostly fresh or previously cooked vegetables, topped with a dressing.

I love to use very simple ingredients, and I found that the fewer the ingredients, the better the salad; and I liked it best when I was still able to identify each individual ingredient on my plate. Too many elements chopped too finely made the meal taste all the same. For convenience, I was constrained by what was available in any grocery store or supermarket and what was in season, but I also wanted to use the occasional fancy ingredient—something unusual, unexpected, or just a bit more expensive to treat myself, like truffle oil, saffron, or caviar.

I tried to come up with rules. More leaves, less meat, more vegetables or fruit, and less cheese, more beans and fewer carbs, more nuts, and less salt. As soon as I created a rule, though, I immediately wanted to change it or disobey it. You'll see how many times I have broken the rules, but it's a good idea, nonetheless, to start with some guidelines and boundaries.

1. Base

1.

2. Vegetables & fruit

2.

3. Protein

3.

4. Toppings

5. Fresh herbs

6. Dressing & spices

4.   5.   6.

HOW TO ASSEMBLE A SALAD

When composing a salad, I divide it into different layers: base, vegetables and fruit, protein, toppings, fresh herbs, and dressings and spices. These are the main ingredients but as you will see, often one (sometimes two) of them is missing. It's up to you to choose what you want to put in it and to enjoy what you are eating. Because these salads are simple assembly jobs, throughout the book I've listed the ingredients that went into each one but no instructions are supplied.

If you are a strict vegetarian, vegan, or "rawist," please check carefully that the ingredients you buy comply with these diets. I've included plenty of cheeses in the vegetarian salads because some vegetarians choose to eat cheese, and because there is a growing number of rennet-free cheeses available, but do replace them if necessary. For raw diets, make sure nuts, dried fruit, etc. have been produced within the necessary temperature limitations of strictly raw products.

The base usually takes up to 50% of your salad—in volume not in weight, as leafy greens are usually quite light. It can be made with salad greens, but also with pasta, grains, potatoes, or even veggie "noodles" like shaved carrots or zucchini ribbons.

25% of the salad should be composed of vegetables and/or fruits, preferably fresh and raw, but they can be also be roasted, steamed, boiled, dried like sun-dried tomatoes, or preserved in olive oil like tomatoes, peppers, or eggplants.

On top of this you might add some protein. You can get your proteins from a very broad range of sources, not just from meat—see page 19. In order to have a balanced diet, proteins shouldn't take over your plate but they should provide a bit of additional flavor.

Next, you can use some toppings to boost the overall taste and texture of the salad: for example pickled vegetables or olives, croutons, or toasted nuts and seeds, but I would say no more than a handful of these (roughly 2 tablespoons).

To top it all, I always love to add some fresh herbs. And finally, I end with the dressing. Never underestimate it. It's like the sauce for the pasta and it can transform your mix of assorted vegetables into a feast.

1. THE BASE

Salad greens are actually the most recognizable element of a salad, i.e., the first association your mind will make as soon as you say the word "salad." There are so many different leaves, from arugula to iceberg (not one of my favorites); from the bitter radicchio to the mild gems of romaine; from baby spinach to red oakleaf lettuce; from tender mâche to spicy watercress.

I love their crispness and freshness—so deliciously satisfying. I like to use raw winter leaves as well, like cabbage, bok choy, kale, or chard because they are crunchy and spicy. If you want them slightly softer, wash them in warm water or massage them with lemon juice. Sometimes I use vegetables, not just leaves, as a base. I like anything that can be chopped finely like cauliflower, or shaved into "spaghetti" or ribbons like carrots, zucchini, parsnips, cucumber, or asparagus. A vegetable peeler, grater, or mandoline will do the job, and it will look very cool, too! I've learned all these ways of preparing vegetables from raw vegan cuisine. Do wash or peel the vegetables first, as you prefer.

I love to use grains as well since they are filling, add texture, and offer another delicious element to salads. This is one of the few ingredients I bring from home. When I cook some pasta, rice, quinoa, or any other grain for dinner (and that happens quite often), I cook some extra for myself for the next day. I leave it aside to cool, then I store it in the refrigerator, and usually I add a sprinkle of olive oil to prevent it from becoming sticky. I love white rice but I find salads work better with less sticky, whole-wheat varieties like brown, red, black, and wild rice. Barley, spelt, and quinoa work very well, too. And I am mad about couscous. We never ate it in Italy, so it was a fantastic discovery for me, as were all the grains, spices, and ingredients of Middle Eastern cuisine. I make couscous all the time in the office. It's so easy, it's like making tea! I take a big tea cup, fill it one-third of the way up with couscous, and add a pinch of salt and a dash of olive oil. Then I pour boiling water in, to just cover the couscous, cover the cup with a cloth, and let it sit for 5 to 10 minutes. Job done.

2. VEGETABLES & FRUIT

Vegetables should take up 25% of your salad, not just because we are advised to eat at least five pieces of fruit and vegetable a day, but because they are good, tasty and full of color, vitamins, minerals, and fiber. I usually try to use two vegetables or fruits on my salads, just to have a bit of variety, but I can use more or less. I love big chunks rather than superfine ones: I relish each ingredient and like to be able to recognize the different pieces in my mouthful of salad.

If I can, I prefer to keep vegetables raw, as their distinctive flavor remains intact and they keep all their nutritional value, vitamins, and nutrients. Fruits look gorgeous in salads, and they pair up so well with cheese. I like to mix two of them together, which is a very safe option. I also like to mix and match raw vegetables with fruits, which can result in very interesting and exotic combinations! Avocado, for instance, can create different effects in a salad, as it can provide firm chunks, or be so yielding and creamy that it acts almost as a dressing.

I don't use cooked fruits in salads. It's not a cake, right? On the other hand, I am very fond of incorporating dried fruits but I'll talk about them later, in the toppings section on page 21. The second best option is to steam the vegetables. Usually, I do it the night before as part of my dinner and I keep the leftovers in the refrigerator until the next day. Another, lengthier option is to roast them. I like to chop the vegetables, add a bit of spice, salt, and oil, and throw them in a hot oven for 30 to 40 minutes until golden and soft. You can fry them in a pan or a wok too, but it's something I don't do that often.

My favorite vegetables to use raw are cucumbers, bell peppers, tomatoes, red onions, carrots, celery, zucchini, radishes, beets, cauliflower, broccoli, fennel, parsnip, asparagus, green beans, and shallots. I've probably left some out!
My favorite vegetables to steam are butternut squash, artichokes, sweet potatoes, broccoli, asparagus, green beans, peas, Jerusalem artichokes, and new potatoes.
My favorite vegetables to roast are bell peppers, butternut squash, onions, artichokes, sweet potatoes, broccoli, eggplants, asparagus, green beans, peas, pumpkin, Jerusalem artichokes, new potatoes, shallots, and so on.
My favorite fruits are avocado, mango, apples, apricots, blackberries, oranges, blueberries, cherries, figs, grapes, melons, watermelon, nectarines, peaches, pears, plums, raspberries, red currants, and strawberries.

3. PROTEIN

One cup, or 25%, of your salad should be dedicated to proteins, which also enhance the flavor of the salad. Don't forget that you can get protein from a wide range of ingredients. Depending on your dietary requirements and your tastes, you can get it from meat (chicken, duck, goose, lamb, turkey, beef, pork); seafood (cod, tuna, crab, sole, haddock, herring, lobster, mackerel, shrimp, salmon, sardines, scallops, sea bass, trout, squid, octopus); eggs; cheese (mozzarella, ricotta, Parmesan, Brie, cottage cheese, goat cheese, Cheddar, Gorgonzola, other blue cheese, halloumi, Gouda, Manchego); soy products such as tofu; beans (lentils, pinto, kidney, black beans, cannellini beans, fava beans, mung beans, chickpeas); grains (quinoa, wheat, couscous, rice, amaranth, barley, rye, oats, buckwheat); or even nuts and seeds (hemp, almonds, Brazil nuts, hazelnuts, walnuts, cashews, pine nuts, pistachios, pumpkin seeds, sesame seeds). Surprised? I often use two different types of protein in my salad—a nut and a cheese, a seed and a fish, a cheese and some meat.

Occasionally I go for raw fish, such as salmon or tuna. This is sometimes called sashimi fish, and you should buy it from a reliable fish supplier and tell him or her that you plan to eat it raw, so that you know you're getting the freshest and best-quality fish. A note on sustainability: I only buy fish and shrimp if I know they have been responsibly sourced. I don't want to contribute to the depletion of fish stocks, and we all have a responsibility to care about where our food comes from and how it's been acquired. For more information, visit the Marine Stewardship Council at www.msc.org and MarineBio Conservation Society at marinebio.org. The same principle applies to all ingredients made from animal products (e.g., eggs, cheese, and meat); I would recommend you buy the best quality you can afford and that it's cage-free, organic, and fair trade when possible.

I always store nuts and leftover canned ingredients in a well sealed container in my drawer or the refrigerator when necessary. (I always fear mice!) I would keep the amount of protein ingredients below the 25% mark, otherwise your plate becomes chicken with a salad on the side, instead of salad with a bit of chicken.

4. TOPPINGS

I call toppings all those salty, nutty, and sweet extra ingredients you need just a tablespoon or two of to brighten the overall combination of your meal.

Nuts and seeds are not just a great source of protein, they taste incredibly good, are full of good fats, and they add extra crunchiness to the whole dish. Some nuts and seeds are better soaked overnight, especially almonds. Others are amazing toasted, like sesame seeds, pumpkin seeds, cashews, and pine nuts. Some of my favorites are hemp, almonds, pecans, hazelnuts, walnuts, cashews, pine nuts, pistachios, pumpkin seeds, sesame seeds, poppy seeds, and flax seeds, to name a few.

I love to use pickled vegetables such as olives, capers, gherkins, pearl onions, and so on, as they boost the savoriness of the salad. Alternatively, I like to use dried fruits such as apricots, dates, raisins, prunes, blueberries to enhance the sweet accents.

5. FRESH HERBS

I always try to add a handful of fresh herbs such as basil, chives, cilantro, dill, mint, oregano, parsley, rosemary, sage, tarragon, thyme (or even sprouted beans) in my salads. They are an essential part of all my recipes; they are the touch that makes a boring salad a rich and synesthetic experience with their amazing smell and taste. I've learned this from Yotam Ottolenghi, who is a salad master! I love to buy pots of fresh herbs, especially basil, parsley, and mint, which last longer and look good as well. Luckily my desk is by the window.

6. DRESSINGS & SPICES

The dressing is where the real magic happens, and the stage at which a salad comes to life. In all your dressings you want to balance some sweet oiliness (oil or nuts), some sourness (vinegar, soy sauce, or citrus juices), and bit of saltiness and spice. Leafy salads should only be dressed just before serving since the dressing will "cook" your leaves and they will become dark and soggy if left too long. Grain and cabbage salads are the opposite and become better when you leave them to absorb the dressing.

Dried herbs, spices, and other ingredients (basil, chives, cilantro, dill, mint, oregano, parsley, rosemary, sage, tarragon, thyme, truffles, nori seaweed, turmeric, curry powder, saffron, fennel, nutmeg, cardamom, cumin, coriander, pepper, cayenne pepper, bay, cinnamon, mustard seeds, garlic, wasabi, ginger, galangal, kaffir lime leaves, marjoram, paprika, sumac) play an important role in the direction you want your salad to go. It's not just about salt and pepper. There are a lot of fantastic spices that can boost your dressing. Don't be too generous as you will taste them much more keenly than you would in a cooked dish. Half a teaspoon is usually enough.

Spices are also really good at complementing the seasons. Spices and herbs are great in the summer when it's hot, as they can cool you down: mint, basil, fennel, cilantro, and tarragon all work well, as they are fresh. Conversely, I use spices in dressings to warm myself up. Black pepper, cayenne, cinnamon, ginger, horseradish (or wasabi), mustard, chili, and paprika are some of my favorites.

There are many different types of dressings, but I divide them into three categories: oily (vinaigrette-style), creamy, and pesto. On the following pages are some of my most-loved ones, and you can choose any of these, or you can simply follow the dressing suggestions given in each salad recipe. You either just mix them together with a fork or whisk, or occasionally you need to blend the ingredients together—I have a tiny little blender (designed for baby purees) that I use.

VINAIGRETTE-STYLE DRESSINGS

CLASSIC ITALIAN

Mix 2 tablespoons extra virgin olive oil, 1 teaspoon balsamic vinegar, and a pinch of salt and pepper

WASABI & SOY SAUCE

Mix 1 tablespoon toasted sesame oil, 1 tablespoon dark soy sauce, 1 teaspoon wasabi powder, and 1 teaspoon canola oil

CITRUS

Mix 2 tablespoons extra virgin olive oil, 1 teaspoon orange juice, 1 teaspoon lemon juice, and a pinch of salt

LEMON ZEST

Mix 2 tablespoons extra virgin olive oil, 2 teaspoons lemon juice, a pinch of salt, and a sprinkle of grated lemon zest

CHILI

Mix 2 tablespoons extra virgin olive oil, 1 teaspoon cider vinegar, a pinch of salt, and 1 to 2 pinches of chili powder

TRUFFLE

Mix 2 tablespoons extra virgin olive oil, 1 teaspoon truffle-infused olive oil, 1 teaspoon balsamic vinegar, and a pinch of salt and pepper

PESTO DRESSINGS

CLASSIC PESTO

Blend together 2 tablespoons extra virgin olive oil, a pinch of salt and pepper, 1 handful of fresh basil leaves, 1 tablespoon pine nuts, 1 tablespoon grated Parmesan cheese, and ¼ garlic clove

OLIVE TAPENADE

Blend together 2 tablespoons extra virgin olive oil, 1 teaspoon cider vinegar, a pinch of salt and pepper, and 2 tablespoons pitted black or green olives

ARTICHOKE PESTO

Blend together 2 teaspoons extra virgin olive oil, 1 teaspoon artichoke purée, 1 teaspoon cider vinegar, and a pinch of salt

RASPBERRY PESTO

Blend together 2 tablespoons extra virgin olive oil, 1 teaspoon lemon juice, a pinch of salt and pepper, and a handful of raspberries

RAW GREEN PESTO

Blend together 2 tablespoons extra virgin olive oil, a pinch of salt and pepper, a handful of fresh herbs (e.g., basil, cilantro, parsley), 1 tablespoon nuts (e.g., pine nuts, cashews, walnuts, almonds, pistachios), and 1 tablespoon water

TOMATO PESTO

Blend together 1 teaspoon sun-dried tomatoe, 1 tablespoon pine nuts, 2 teaspoons extra virgin olive oil, 1 teaspoon cider vinegar, and a pinch of salt and pepper

CREAMY DRESSINGS

NUT & LEMON

Blend together 2 teaspoons extra virgin olive oil, 1 teaspoon lemon juice, a pinch of salt, 2 teaspoons nuts (e.g., almonds, cashews, walnuts), and 1 teaspoon water

TOASTED SESAME

Blend together 2 tablespoons extra virgin olive oil, 1 teaspoon cider vinegar, 1 teaspoon tahini, a pinch of salt, and 2 tablespoons toasted sesame seeds

THAI CURRY

Blend together 2 tablespoons soy cream or coconut cream, 1 tablespoon unsweetened shredded coconut, and 1 teaspoon Thai green curry paste

VEGAN COCONUT & GINGER

Blend together 2 tablespoons soy cream or coconut cream, 1 teaspoon coconut water or milk, 2 tablespoons unsweetened shredded coconut, and 1 teaspoon ground ginger

ENGLISH MUSTARD

Mix 2 tablespoons extra virgin olive oil, 1 tablespoon mayonnaise, 1 teaspoon English mustard, and a pinch of salt

CREAM & SPICES

Mix 1 teaspoon ground spice (e.g., smoked paprika, chili powder, cumin, ginger, turmeric), 2 tablespoons light cream, and a pinch of salt

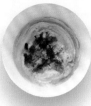

HUMMUS

Mix 2 tablespoons extra virgin olive oil, 2 tablespoons hummus, 1 teaspoon lemon juice, a pinch of salt and pepper, and 2 pinches of smoked paprika

RAW NUT & AGAVE

Blend together 2 tablespoons extra virgin olive oil, 2 tablespoons cashews, a pinch of salt, 1 teaspoon water, and 1 teaspoon agave nectar

SAFFRON MAYO

Mix 2 tablespoons mayonnaise, 1 teaspoon cider vinegar, a pinch of saffron threads, and a pinch of salt

FRENCH MUSTARD

Blend together 2 tablespoons extra virgin olive oil, 1 teaspoon cider vinegar, a pinch of salt and pepper, 1 teaspoon light cream, and 1 teaspoon whole-grain Dijon mustard

TARTARE

Blend together 1 teaspoon capers, 2 teaspoons extra virgin olive oil, 1 teaspoon lemon juice, 2 tablespoons plain yogurt, a pinch of salt and pepper, and 1 tablespoon fresh parsley leaves

RAW PINE NUT "MAYO"

Blend together 2 teaspoons extra virgin olive oil, 2 teaspoons pine nuts, a pinch of salt, 1 teaspoon water, and 1 teaspoon ground turmeric

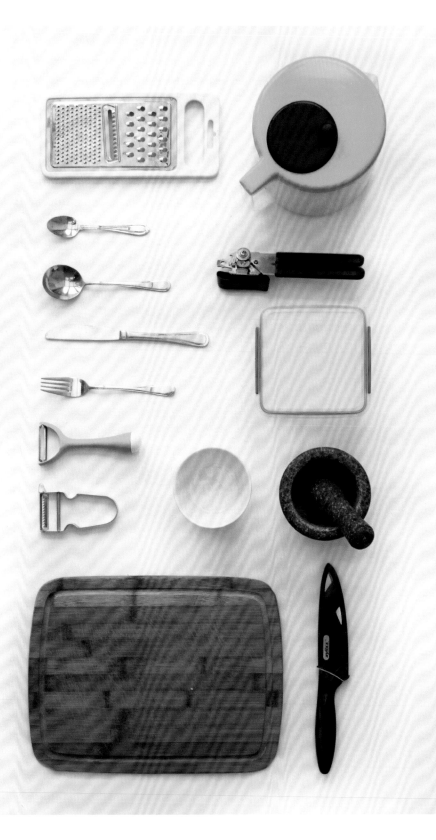

MY TOOLS

You can't have a whole kitchen for you in the office, but you need a series of basic tools to be able to create a good, fresh salad. First you need a cutting board and a knife; without those it is quite hard to function effectively. I always suggest having a proper kitchen knife on hand. It makes the chopping easier, quicker, and more precise.

One of my favorite tools is the vegetable peeler. Use it to peel vegetables and fruits, of course, but also learn to use it to shave into ribbons or flakes hard cheeses such as Parmesan and pecorino or vegetables such as zucchini, cucumber, carrots, and parsnips. If you want to simulate "spaghetti," use a julienne peeler and the ribbons magically become thinner strips.

Another essential tool is the salad spinner, a compact version of which fits in my desk drawer. I always recommend that you wash even prewashed packed lettuce. Wet salad bags are bacteria heaven! I use a little bowl or jar that I use to mix dressings. In the beginning I had measuring spoons, but now I don't use them anymore as my eye is trained enough to gauge size and weight with a glance. Like my mom used to say: "you need enough of that ingredient," to which I would reply "how much is enough?" And she used to say "when it's enough, you'll see it, you'll know it." She used to cook divinely.

I always have a collection of airtight boxes in different sizes. I often use less than a package of cheese, meat, or ham in any one salad and store the leftovers for the next day. I try to plan ahead when I go food shopping. For example, I might buy 3½ ounces of cheese to use in at least two recipes over the next few days.

Other tools I have that you might like to equip yourself with: can opener, strainer, latex gloves (for chopping beet or red cabbage!), mortar and pestle, grater, and scissors. I have them all, and my drawer is almost exploding. I have a sprout germinator, too, and everything needed for washing my plate and utensils at the end of lunch.

A YEAR OF SALADS

I've learned a lot in my journey creating daily lunch salads, a journey that has included some failures but mostly successes. I believe more than ever that salads are a great meal. For three years, I succeeded in creating a lunch at my desk every single day. I've discovered how good my own rich, gorgeous, and tasty salads can be, and how easy to prepare. At the end of it all, I am just as much in love with salads as when I started. It really hurts me when I see them being treated simply as a sad and unsexy little side dish, or a prelude to the main event. Salads can be beautiful and bright, healthy and tasty, a fulfilling and complete meal. In conducting this experiment, I've tried to give salads and healthy eating a new and more appealing image.

I know that I am not alone: I've seen a lot of people changing their diets and embracing healthier habits around me in my office, in London, and around the world. The perception about salads and healthy food has changed. I've seen colleagues of mine creating Salad Clubs, preparing their fresh salads at their desks or in communal areas. At the same time, by eating these yummy, vitamin- and mineral-rich creations, I feel I've changed my body, my appearance, and my point of view about food in general. After these days, weeks, months, and years of creating salads, I love food now more than ever, and I've never been so enthusiastic about salads. Eating healthily was never meant to be boring or painful; it should and can be a delicious treat to ourselves. In this book I've decided to represent the best examples of my years of salad exploration: the most interesting and outrageous, the most innovative and successful.

The recipes in this book are real meals, photographed just a few seconds before being devoured. They were all assembled in no more than 20 minutes (although some required ingredients to be precooked, either by you the night before or by a deli or supermarket). They are divided by season and cover five different dietary requirements—raw, vegan, vegetarian, pescatarian, and omnivore.

There is a salad for everyone, for any time, any mood, and any budget. I've also added an "alternative" to each one to help you convert it for a different diet, or just to make it lighter or richer depending on your mood. I hope I can fire your imagination and inspire you to create different, new, and even more interesting combinations. Buon appetito!

RAW ALTERNATIVE

Replace the mozzarella with 1 ripe avocado and ¼ red onion

MOZZARELLA, CHERRY TOMATOES & SPINACH

For the salad, assemble:

2 ounces baby spinach
1⅓ cups cherry tomatoes, halved
½ cup chopped mozzarella
Handful of fresh basil leaves

For the dressing, mix:

1 tablespoon extra virgin olive oil
1 teaspoon balsamic vinegar
Pinch of salt and pepper
Pinch of dried oregano

CRABMEAT, CHERRY TOMATOES & WATERCRESS

For the salad, assemble:

2 ounces watercress
⅔ cup cherry tomatoes, halved
2 ounces cooked crabmeat
Handful of pine nuts
Handful of fresh flat-leaf parsley leaves

For the dressing, mix:

1 tablespoon extra virgin olive oil
1 teaspoon balsamic vinegar
Pinch of salt and pepper

VEGETARIAN
ALTERNATIVE

*Add 3¹/₂ ounces feta or
goat cheese*

BLACK GRAPES, MELON & HEMP CREAM

For the salad, assemble:

1 head of Boston lettuce
3¹/₂ ounces honeydew, chopped
Handful of black grapes
1 tablespoon shelled hemp seeds
Handful of fresh mint leaves

For the dressing, blend together:

1 tablespoon extra virgin olive oil
1 teaspoon lemon juice
Pinch of salt and pepper
Handful of shelled hemp seeds

RAW ALTERNATIVE

Replace the yogurt with the Raw Nut & Agave dressing on page 27, made with almonds

STRAWBERRIES, MELON & ALMONDS

For the salad, assemble:

2 ounces red oakleaf lettuce
Scant ¾ cup strawberries, hulled and chopped
3½ ounces cantaloupe, chopped
Handful of almonds, chopped
Handful of fresh mint leaves

For the dressing, mix:

Scant ¼ cup plain yogurt
1 tablespoon extra virgin olive oil
Pinch of salt and pepper

HONEY-ROASTED SALMON, FENNEL & SPINACH

For the salad, assemble:

2 ounces baby spinach
½ fennel bulb, thinly sliced
⅔ cup cherry tomatoes, halved
2 ounces honey-roasted salmon, flaked
Handful of pumpkin seeds
Handful of fresh flat-leaf parsley leaves

For the dressing, mix:

1 tablespoon extra virgin olive oil
1 teaspoon lemon juice
Pinch of salt and pepper

PROSCIUTTO, PARMESAN & CHERRY TOMATOES

For the salad, assemble:

2 ounces arugula
1 cup cherry tomatoes, halved
2 ounces prosciutto, roughly shredded
1 cup Parmesan cheese shavings

For the dressing, mix:

1 tablespoon extra virgin olive oil
1 teaspoon balsamic vinegar
Pinch of salt and pepper

RAW

OMNIVORE
ALTERNATIVE
*Add 2 ounces chorizo
or pastrami*

PURPLE CARROT, RED PEPPER & CHILE PESTO

For the salad, assemble:

*2 small purple (or orange) carrots, shaved into
ribbons with a vegetable peeler*
½ Italian sweet red pepper, diced
Handful of fresh mint leaves

For the dressing, blend together:

1 tablespoon extra virgin olive oil
1 teaspoon cider vinegar
Pinch of salt and pepper
½ red chile, chopped
*Handful of cashews (soaked overnight
if preferred)*

SWEET POTATO, RED CABBAGE & CHERRY TOMATOES

For the salad, assemble:

Generous 1 cup finely shredded red cabbage
½ baked sweet potato, peeled and chopped
⅔ cup cherry tomatoes, quartered
2 scallions, finely chopped
1 tablespoon sesame seeds

For the dressing, mix:

1 tablespoon extra virgin olive oil
1 teaspoon lemon juice
Pinch of salt and pepper
2 tablespoons hummus

CHICKPEAS, COUSCOUS & CHERRY TOMATOES

For the salad, assemble:

Scant ²/₃ cup cooked couscous
²/₃ cup canned chickpeas
²/₃ cup cherry tomatoes, quartered
1 teaspoon toasted sesame seeds
Handful of pitted black olives, halved
Handful of fresh flat-leaf parsley leaves

For the dressing, mix:

1 tablespoon extra virgin olive oil
1 teaspoon cider vinegar
Pinch of salt and pepper

OMNIVORE

VEGAN
ALTERNATIVE
*Replace the spicy roasted
chicken with 3½ ounces
steamed green beans*

CHICKEN, NEW POTATOES & CHERRY TOMATOES

For the salad, assemble:

2 ounces arugula
⅔ cup cherry tomatoes, halved
3½ ounces roasted new potatoes, halved
2 ounces roasted spicy chicken, chopped
Handful of fresh flat-leaf parsley leaves

For the dressing, mix:

1 tablespoon extra virgin olive oil
1 teaspoon balsamic vinegar
Pinch of salt and pepper

PEAS & ROASTED SWEET POTATO & EGGPLANT

For the salad, assemble:

½ cup cooked brown basmati rice
Scant ⅓ cup steamed peas
3½ ounces roasted sweet potato, chopped
½ cubed and roasted eggplant
Handful of cashews
Handful of fresh cilantro leaves

For the dressing, mix:

1 tablespoon extra virgin olive oil
1 teaspoon cider vinegar
Pinch of salt and pepper
2 pinches of curry powder

PESCATARIAN

OMINVORE ALTERNATIVE

Replace the shrimp with 2 ounces roasted chicken

SHRIMP, BABY CORN & SUGAR SNAP PEAS

For the salad, assemble:

½ cup cooked brown short-grain rice
2 ounces raw (or lightly steamed) baby corn
2 ounces raw (or steamed) sugar snap peas
Handful of fresh cilantro leaves
Handful of cooked shrimp

For the dressing, blend together:

2 tablespoons soy cream or coconut cream
1 teaspoon coconut water or milk
2 tablespoons unsweetened shredded coconut
2 pinches of dried red pepper flakes
Pinch of salt

GREEN BEANS, PARMESAN & PINE NUTS

For the salad, assemble:

2 ounces arugula
2 ounces steamed green beans
1 cup Parmesan cheese shavings
Handful of pine nuts
Handful of whole-wheat croutons
Handful of fresh basil leaves
Bunch of garlic sprouts

For the dressing, mix:

1 tablespoon extra virgin olive oil
1 teaspoon balsamic vinegar
Pinch of salt and pepper

CRABMEAT, AVOCADO, NORI & CUCUMBER

For the salad, assemble:

2 ounces watercress

1 avocado, chopped

¾ cup chopped cucumber

2 ounces cooked crabmeat

1 sheet of nori (toasted seaweed), thinly sliced

1 teaspoon toasted sesame seeds

For the dressing, mix:

1 tablespoon sunflower oil

1 teaspoon light soy sauce

Pinch of salt and pepper

Pinch of wasabi powder

CHICKEN, BLUE CHEESE & CHERRY TOMATOES

For the salad, assemble:

2 ounces arugula
Handful of cherry tomatoes, quartered
2 ounces roasted chicken, chopped
Generous ¼ cup chopped blue cheese

For the dressing, mix:

1 tablespoon extra virgin olive oil
1 teaspoon balsamic vinegar
Pinch of salt
Pinch of dried red pepper flakes

NEW POTATOES, GREEN BEANS & BLACK OLIVES

For the salad, assemble:

3½ ounces chopped and steamed new potatoes
2 ounces steamed green beans
⅔ cup cherry tomatoes, halved
Handful of pitted black olives
½ very small red onion, thinly sliced

For the dressing, blend together:

2 handfuls of fresh basil leaves
2 teaspoons extra virgin olive oil
Handful of pine nuts
¼ garlic clove
1 teaspoon cider vinegar

BLACK LENTILS, COUSCOUS & PECORINO

For the salad, assemble:

Scant ⅔ cup cooked couscous
⅓ cup canned black lentils
Scant ⅔ cup pecorino shavings
*3 to 4 fresh chive flowers (or a bunch of chives,
   chopped)*
Bunch of fresh flat-leaf parsley leaves

For the dressing, mix:

*1 tablespoon artichoke purée (or handful of
   marinated artichoke hearts, blended)*
1 tablespoon extra virgin olive oil
1 teaspoon balsamic vinegar
Pinch of salt and pepper

RAW ALTERNATIVE

Replace the croutons with some nuts or seeds, or just omit them; add raw olives

CHERRY TOMATOES, BLACK OLIVES & BORAGE FLOWERS

For the salad, assemble:

2 ounces mixed salad greens (e.g., watercress, red chard, and mâche)
⅔ cup cherry tomatoes, halved
½ small cucumber, chopped
2 scallions, chopped
Handful of pitted black olives, halved
Handful of croutons
Handful of pine nuts
Handful of borage flowers

For the dressing, mix:

1 tablespoon extra virgin olive oil
1 teaspoon cider vinegar
Pinch of salt and pepper

51

FETA, WATERMELON & FENNEL

For the salad, assemble:

2 ounces arugula
3½ ounces watermelon, seeded and chopped
½ fennel bulb, thinly sliced
Handful of pomegranate seeds
Generous ¼ cup chopped feta
Handful of pumpkin seeds
Handful of fresh dill fronds

For the dressing, mix:

1 tablespoon extra virgin olive oil
1 teaspoon lemon juice
Pinch of salt and pepper

CHICORY, STRAWBERRIES & FENNEL

For the salad, assemble:

1 head of red chicory, thinly sliced
½ small fennel bulb, thinly sliced
Scant ¾ cup strawberries, hulled and chopped
1 tablespoon pumpkin seeds
Handful of fresh mint leaves

For the dressing, mix:

1 tablespoon extra virgin olive oil
1 teaspoon lemon juice
Pinch of salt and pepper

VEGAN ALTERNATIVE

Add a handful of croutons to the chopped tomatoes and let them soak for 10 minutes

ZUCCHINI, CHERRY TOMATOES & AVOCADO

For the salad, assemble:

1 zucchini, shaved into ribbons with a vegetable peeler
3½ ounces black (or regular) cherry tomatoes, quartered
1 avocado, chopped
1 teaspoon shelled hemp seeds
Handful of fresh chives, chopped

For the dressing, mix:

1 tablespoon extra virgin olive oil
1 teaspoon balsamic vinegar
Pinch of salt and pepper

PROSCIUTTO, MELON & CROUTONS

For the salad, assemble:

2 ounces arugula
2 ounces prosciutto, roughly shredded
Handful of croutons
Handful of fresh chives, chopped
3½ ounces cantaloupe, chopped

For the dressing, mix:

1 tablespoon extra virgin olive oil
1 teaspoon balsamic vinegar
Pinch of salt and pepper

COTTAGE CHEESE, PEAS & CUCUMBER

For the salad, assemble:

2 ounces arugula and baby watercress
Scant ⅓ cup steamed peas
Generous ⅓ cup chopped cucumber
Scant ¼ cup cottage cheese
2 scallions, finely chopped

For the dressing, mix:

1 tablespoon extra virgin olive oil
1 teaspoon cider vinegar
Pinch of salt and pepper

RAW
ALTERNATIVE
*Replace the anchovies
with a handful of capers,
and use raw olives*

ANCHOVIES, CUCUMBER, RED PEPPER & BLACK OLIVES

For the salad, assemble:

3½ ounces cucumber, shredded with a julienne peeler
½ Italian sweet red pepper, diced
2 ounces marinated anchovies
Handful of pitted black olives, halved
Handful of pine nuts
Handful of fresh flat-leaf parsley leaves

For the dressing, mix:

1 tablespoon extra virgin olive oil
1 teaspoon cider vinegar
Pinch of salt and pepper

OMNIVORE

VEGETARIAN ALTERNATIVE

Replace the bresaola
with salty cheese, such as
Quartirolo Lombardo
or feta

BRESAOLA, NECTARINE & CASHEWS

For the salad, assemble:

2 ounces mixed salad greens
2 nectarines, cut into wedges
2 ounces bresaola (air-dried beef), thinly sliced
Handful of cashews
Handful of fresh mint leaves

For the dressing, mix:

1 tablespoon extra virgin olive oil
1 teaspoon balsamic vinegar
Pinch of salt and pepper

OAK-SMOKED CHEDDAR, PEACHES & BLUEBERRIES

For the salad, assemble:

*2 ounces mixed baby salad greens (e.g., chard, spinach,
   and red oakleaf lettuce)*
2 small peaches, sliced
Handful of blueberries
Generous ¼ cup cubed oak-smoked Cheddar cheese
Handful of walnuts, chopped
Handful of fresh mint leaves

For the dressing, mix:

1 tablespoon extra virgin olive oil
1 teaspoon balsamic vinegar
Pinch of salt and pepper

OMNIVORE

VEGETARIAN
ALTERNATIVE
*Replace the smoked
ham with canned beans
or chickpeas and add
more tomatoes*

SMOKED HAM, SCAMORZA & PISTACHIOS

For the salad, assemble:

*2¼ ounces mixed salad greens (e.g., watercress, red
    oakleaf lettuce, and arugula)*
⅔ cup cherry tomatoes, halved
2 ounces smoked ham, thinly sliced
Generous ¼ cup cubed scamorza (smoked cheese)
Handful of pistachios

For the dressing, mix:

1 tablespoon extra virgin olive oil
1 teaspoon balsamic vinegar
Pinch of salt and pepper

GOAT CHEESE, RED PEPPER & PINE NUTS

For the salad, assemble:

2 ounces arugula
¹/₂ red bell pepper, chopped
Generous ¹/₄ cup chopped firm goat cheese
Handful of pine nuts

For the dressing, mix:

1 tablespoon extra virgin olive oil
1 teaspoon balsamic vinegar
Pinch of salt and pepper
1 tablespoon Tomato Pesto (page 25)

VEGAN

RAW ALTERNATIVE
Replace the hummus with a raw hummus-style dip or a ripe avocado

RED PEPPER, WATERCRESS & PINE NUTS

For the salad, assemble:

2¼ ounces watercress
1 Italian sweet red pepper, finely chopped
Handful of pine nuts
Bunch of fresh chives, chopped

For the dressing, mix:

1 tablespoon extra virgin olive oil
1 teaspoon balsamic vinegar
Pinch of salt and pepper
1 tablespoon red pepper hummus

RAW

OMNIVORE ALTERNATIVE
Add 3½ ounces roasted chicken or turkey, pastrami, or smoked ham

RED & YELLOW PEPPERS, ZUCCHINI & RAISINS

For the salad, assemble:

1 zucchini, shaved into ribbons with a vegetable peeler
½ Italian sweet red pepper, thinly sliced
½ Italian sweet yellow pepper, thinly sliced
Handful of raisins
Handful of pine nuts
Handful of fresh chives, chopped

For the dressing, mix:

1 tablespoon extra virgin olive oil
1 teaspoon cider vinegar
Pinch of salt and pepper

CHORIZO, GREEN OLIVES & WHOLE-WHEAT PASTA

For the salad, assemble:

3½ ounces cooked whole-wheat penne
⅔ cup cherry tomatoes, halved
2 ounces chorizo, chopped
Handful of pitted green olives
2 scallions, thinly sliced
Handful of fresh flat-leaf parsley leaves

For the dressing, mix:

1 tablespoon extra virgin olive oil
1 teaspoon balsamic vinegar
Pinch of salt and pepper
2 pinches of dried red pepper flakes

ROASTED PEPPERS, CHICKPEAS & BARLEY

For the salad, assemble:

Scant ⅔ cup cooked barley
1 chopped and roasted red and/or yellow bell pepper
⅔ cup canned chickpeas
Handful of pitted black olives
Handful of fresh flat-leaf parsley leaves

For the dressing, mix:

1 tablespoon extra virgin olive oil
1 teaspoon balsamic vinegar
Pinch of salt and pepper

ROASTED SALMON, SPELT, ZUCCHINI & RED PEPPER

For the salad, assemble:

1 zucchini, shaved into ribbons with a vegetable peeler
1 red bell pepper, sliced
¼ cup cooked spelt, barley, or brown basmati rice
2 ounces roasted salmon, flaked
Handful of fresh flat-leaf parsley leaves

For the dressing, mix:

1 tablespoon extra virgin olive oil
1 teaspoon cider vinegar
Pinch of salt and pepper

ROASTED EGGPLANT, PEPPERS & ZUCCHINI

For the salad, assemble:

½ small zucchini, shaved into ribbons with a vegetable peeler
½ small sliced and roasted eggplant
Handful of marinated peppers from a jar
1 teaspoon crispy onions
Bunch of fresh chives, chopped

For the dressing, mix:

1 tablespoon extra virgin olive oil
1 teaspoon balsamic vinegar
Pinch of salt and pepper

VEGAN

OMNIVORE ALTERNATIVE
Add some roasted chicken or a handful of cooked shrimp

GREEN BEANS, RED PEPPER, WILD RICE & CHILE

For the salad, assemble:

Generous 1 cup cooked wild rice
3½ ounces steamed green beans
½ red bell pepper, sliced
2 scallions, thinly sliced
½ small red chile, finely chopped
Handful of fresh baby cilantro and red amaranth leaves

For the dressing, mix:

¾-inch fresh ginger, peeled and grated
2 teaspoons sweet white miso
2 teaspoons oat cream or coconut cream

COUSCOUS, ROASTED CHICKEN & VEGETABLES

For the salad, assemble:

Scant ⅔ cup cooked couscous
2 ounces roasted chicken breast, chopped
3½ ounces roasted vegetables (e.g., ½ eggplant, ½ red
    bell pepper, and ½ yellow bell pepper)
1 teaspoon toasted pine nuts
Handful of fresh flat-leaf parsley leaves

For the dressing, mix:

1 tablespoon extra virgin olive oil
1 teaspoon balsamic vinegar
Pinch of salt and pepper
Pinch of dried marjoram

VEGETARIAN
ALTERNATIVE
*Add some Parmesan
and dress the salad with
balsamic vinegar glaze*

BROCCOLI, STRAWBERRIES & BLUEBERRIES

For the salad, assemble:

*3¼ ounces mixed baby salad greens (e.g., chard,
    watercress, and red oakleaf lettuce)*
1 ounce broccoli, chopped
Handful of strawberries, hulled and quartered
Handful of blueberries
Handful of hazelnuts, chopped

For the dressing, mix:

1 tablespoon extra virgin olive oil
1 teaspoon lemon juice
Pinch of salt and pepper

COTTAGE CHEESE, BLUEBERRIES & SPINACH

For the salad, assemble:

1 ounce arugula
1 ounce baby spinach
⅓ cup blueberries
Scant ½ cup cottage cheese
Handful of toasted pumpkin seeds
Bunch of fresh chives, chopped

For the dressing, mix:

1 tablespoon extra virgin olive oil
1 teaspoon balsamic vinegar
Pinch of salt and pepper

PESCATARIAN
ALTERNATIVE
Add a handful of cooked shrimp or 2 ounces canned tuna (preserved in water)

RED CABBAGE, ZUCCHINI, AVOCADO & WALNUTS

For the salad, assemble:

Generous 1 cup finely shredded red cabbage
1 small zucchini, chopped
1 avocado, chopped
Handful of walnuts, chopped
Handful of fresh chives, chopped

For the dressing, mix:

1 tablespoon extra virgin olive oil
1 teaspoon lemon juice
Pinch of salt and pepper

RAW ALTERNATIVE

Replace the squid with 1 ripe avocado and ¼ red onion, and use untoasted sesame seeds

SQUID, RED CABBAGE, CARROT & BLACK OLIVES

For the salad, assemble:

Generous 1 cup finely shredded red cabbage
*1 small carrot, shaved into ribbons with a
   vegetable peeler*
Handful of cherry tomatoes, chopped
Handful of pitted black olives, halved
2 ounces cooked squid, chopped
1 teaspoon toasted sesame seeds
Bunch of fresh chives, chopped

For the dressing, mix:

1 tablespoon extra virgin olive oil
1 teaspoon lemon juice
Pinch of salt and pepper
Pinch of dried red pepper flakes

OMNIVORE ALTERNATIVE

Add a handful of chorizo slices and toast the pine nuts

ZUCCHINI, NASTURTIUMS & WILD GREENS

For the salad, assemble:

2 ounces mixed wild salad greens (e.g., watercress and arugula)
1 zucchini, chopped
2 purple (or regular) scallions, finely chopped
Handful of pine nuts
Handful of edible red nasturtium flowers

For the dressing, blend together:

1 tablespoon extra virgin olive oil
1 teaspoon lemon juice
Pinch of salt and pepper
1 small chile, chopped

ROASTED CHICKEN, SUGAR SNAP PEAS & NASTURTIUMS

For the salad, assemble:

2 ounces wild arugula
3½ ounces sugar snap peas or snow peas
3½ ounces roasted chicken breast, chopped
Handful of pine nuts
Handful of fresh cilantro leaves
Handful of edible red nasturtium flowers

For the dressing, mix:

1 tablespoon extra virgin olive oil
1 teaspoon lime juice
1 teaspoon toasted sesame oil
Pinch of salt
¾–inch fresh ginger, peeled and grated

VEGETARIAN
ALTERNATIVE

*Replace the shrimp with
2 ounces firm goat cheese,
Brie, or 1 cup pecorino
shavings*

SHRIMP, BABY CORN, TOMATOES & CHILE

For the salad, assemble:

2 ounces arugula
1 tomato, chopped
3½ ounces steamed baby corn
Handful of cooked shrimp
Handful of pumpkin seeds
1 small red chile, finely chopped
Handful of fresh cilantro leaves

For the dressing, mix:

1 tablespoon extra virgin olive oil
1 teaspoon cider vinegar
Pinch of salt and pepper

SUN-DRIED TOMATOES, CORN & LETTUCE

For the salad, assemble:

2¼ ounces baby red oakleaf lettuce
½ cup of fresh or canned corn
6 sun-dried tomatoes, chopped
Handful of pumpkin seeds
Handful of fresh chives, chopped

For the dressing, mix:

1 tablespoon extra virgin olive oil
1 teaspoon cider vinegar
Pinch of salt and pepper

CHORIZO, SPELT, ZUCCHINI & BLACK BEANS

For the salad, assemble:

1 zucchini, shredded with a julienne peeler
Scant $\frac{1}{3}$ cup cooked spelt
$\frac{2}{3}$ cup cherry tomatoes, halved
$\frac{1}{3}$ cup canned black beans
handful of pine nuts
2 ounces chorizo, chopped
2 scallions, chopped

For the dressing, mix:

1 tablespoon extra virgin olive oil
1 teaspoon balsamic vinegar
Pinch of salt and pepper

KIDNEY BEANS, WILD RICE & AVOCADO

For the salad, assemble:

½ cup cooked mixed brown, wild, and red rice
⅔ cup canned kidney beans
½ avocado, chopped
Handful of cherry tomatoes, halved
½ small red onion, finely chopped
Handful of fresh flat-leaf parsley leaves

For the dressing, mix:

1 tablespoon extra virgin olive oil
1 teaspoon cider vinegar
Pinch of salt and pepper

SQUID, OCTOPUS, COUSCOUS & PEAS

For the salad, assemble:

Scant ⅔ cup cooked pearl couscous
Scant ⅓ cup boiled peas
⅔ cup cherry tomatoes, quartered
2 ounces mixed marinated squid and octopus antipasti

For the dressing, mix:

1 tablespoon extra virgin olive oil
1 teaspoon cider vinegar
Pinch of salt and pepper
Pinch of saffron threads

STRAWBERRIES, PARMESAN & RED CHICORY

For the salad, assemble:

1 small head of red chicory
1 cup strawberries, hulled and quartered
1 cup Parmesan cheese shavings
Handful of pine nuts
Bunch of fresh chives, chopped

For the dressing, mix:

1 tablespoon extra virgin olive oil
1 teaspoon balsamic vinegar
Pinch of salt and pepper

OMNIVORE
ALTERNATIVE
*Add 2 ounces roasted
chicken*

YELLOW PEPPER, BROCCOLI, CHILE & COCONUT CREAM

For the salad, assemble:

2 ounces watercress
½ yellow bell pepper, sliced
3½ ounces broccoli, chopped
2 scallions, thinly sliced
½ red chile, finely chopped
Handful of fresh cilantro leaves

For the dressing, mix:

1 tablespoon extra virgin olive oil
1 tablespoon Vegan Coconut & Ginger dressing
  (page 26)
Pinch of salt

CHICKEN, QUINOA, ZUCCHINI & CHERRY TOMATOES

For the salad, assemble:

½ zucchini, shaved into ribbons with a vegetable peeler
Generous ¼ cup cooked black and white quinoa
Handful of cherry tomatoes, chopped
2 scallions, chopped
2 ounces roasted chicken, chopped
Handful of pumpkin seeds
Handful of fresh basil leaves

For the dressing, mix:

1 tablespoon extra virgin olive oil
1 teaspoon balsamic vinegar
Pinch of salt and pepper

RAW

VEGAN ALTERNATIVE
Add 2 ounces smoked tofu

CARROT, SUGAR SNAP PEAS & AVOCADO

For the salad, assemble:

2 ounces wild (or regular) arugula
Handful of sugar snap peas or snow peas
½ carrot, cut into thin sticks
1 avocado, sliced
Handful of pine nuts
3 to 4 edible violet flowers

For the dressing, blend together:

1 tablespoon peanut oil
Pinch of salt
2 tablespoons coconut milk
1 tablespoon unsweetened coconut flakes
¾-inch fresh ginger, peeled and grated

VEGAN

OMNIVORE
ALTERNATIVE
*Replace the sun-dried
tomatoes with 2 ounces
smoked ham*

CANNELLINI BEANS & BABA GHANOUSH

For the salad, assemble:

*2 ounces mixed salad greens (e.g. red oakleaf lettuce,
watercress, and arugula)*
²/₃ cup canned cannellini beans
Handful of sun-dried tomatoes, chopped
2 scallions, thinly sliced
Handful of pine nuts
3 teaspoons baba ghanoush (eggplant dip)
Handful of edible red and yellow nasturtium flowers

For the dressing, mix:

1 tablespoon extra virgin olive oil
1 teaspoon balsamic vinegar
Pinch of salt and pepper

TUNA, CHICKPEAS, GREEN BEANS & RED PEPPERS

For the salad, assemble:

1 red bell pepper, sliced
3½ ounces steamed green beans
½ small red onion, thinly sliced
2 ounces canned tuna (preserved in water), flaked
Handful of canned chickpeas
Handful of fresh flat-leaf parsley leaves

For the dressing, mix:

1 tablespoon extra virgin olive oil
1 teaspoon cider vinegar
Pinch of salt and pepper

ROAST BEEF, QUINOA, ZUCCHINI & MARINATED PEPPERS

For the salad, assemble:

1 zucchini, shredded with a julienne peeler
Generous ¼ cup cooked white quinoa
2 ounces roast beef, thinly sliced
Handful of marinated red peppers from a jar
Handful of pumpkin seeds
Handful of garlic sprouts

For the dressing, mix:

1 tablespoon extra virgin olive oil
1 teaspoon balsamic vinegar
Pinch of salt and pepper

VEGAN

VEGETARIAN
ALTERNATIVE
*Add 1 cup pecorino or
Parmesan shavings*

WHOLE-WHEAT PASTA, CANNELLINI BEANS & TOMATOES

For the salad, assemble:

3¹/₂ ounces cooked whole-wheat fusilli
²/₃ cup canned cannellini beans
²/₃ cup cherry tomatoes, halved
Handful of fresh basil leaves

For the dressing, mix:

1 tablespoon chili-infused extra virgin olive oil
1 teaspoon balsamic vinegar
Pinch of salt and pepper

QUINOA, FETA, PEPPERS & BLACK OLIVES

For the salad, assemble:

½ cup cooked red and white quinoa
½ red bell pepper, diced
½ yellow bell pepper, diced
¼ red onion, diced
Handful of pitted black olives, halved
Generous ¼ cup cubed feta
Handful of fresh flat-leaf parsley leaves

For the dressing, mix:

1 tablespoon extra virgin olive oil
1 teaspoon balsamic vinegar
Pinch of salt and pepper

BLACKBERRIES, MELON & HEMP SEEDS

For the salad, assemble:

2 ounces mixed salad greens
3½ ounces cantaloupe, chopped
Scant ¾ cup blackberries
Handful of shelled hemp seeds
4 edible violet flowers

For the dressing, mix:

1 tablespoon extra virgin olive oil
1 teaspoon lemon juice
Pinch of salt and pepper

RAW ALTERNATIVE

Replace the goat cheese with pomegranate seeds, grapes, or raisins

GOAT CHEESE, MELON, BLUEBERRIES & SPINACH

For the salad, assemble:

2 ounces baby spinach
3½ ounces cantaloupe, chopped
Handful of blueberries
Generous ¼ cup chopped firm goat cheese (or Brie)
1 tablespoon shelled hemp seeds
Handful of fresh mint leaves

For the dressing, mix:

1 tablespoon extra virgin olive oil
1 teaspoon balsamic vinegar
Pinch of salt and pepper

CHICKEN, QUINOA, SUN-DRIED TOMATOES & AVOCADO

For the salad, assemble:

2 ounces watercress
2 ounces cucumber, cut into long thin sticks
Generous ¼ cup cooked red and white quinoa
½ avocado, chopped
Handful of sun-dried tomatoes
2 ounces roasted chicken, sliced
Handful of fresh cilantro leaves

For the dressing, mix:

1 tablespoon extra virgin olive oil
1 teaspoon balsamic vinegar
Pinch of salt and pepper

GOAT CHEESE, KALE, CUCUMBER & TOMATOES

For the salad, assemble:

½ cup finely chopped kale (discard the stems)
3½ ounces cucumber, cut into long thin sticks
½ cup chopped tomatoes
2 ounces firm goat cheese (or Brie), chopped
Handful of pine nuts
Handful of fresh basil leaves

For the dressing, mix:

1 tablespoon extra virgin olive oil
1 teaspoon balsamic vinegar
Pinch of salt and pepper

SALMON, BLACK BEANS & WHOLE-WHEAT PASTA

For the salad, assemble:

3½ ounces cooked whole-wheat penne

⅔ cup canned black beans

⅔ cup cherry tomatoes, halved

2 ounces raw or steamed broccoli, chopped

2 ounces roasted salmon, flaked

2 scallions, chopped

1 teaspoon nori (toasted seaweed) sprinkle

For the dressing, mix:

1 tablespoon extra virgin olive oil

1 teaspoon cider vinegar

Pinch of salt and pepper

VEGAN

VEGETARIAN
ALTERNATIVE
*Add 1 cup pecorino or
Parmesan shavings*

BARLEY, ROASTED EGGPLANT & RED ONION

For the salad, assemble:

Scant ⅔ cup cooked barley
1 finely chopped and roasted eggplant
1 sliced and roasted red onion
Handful of fresh basil leaves

For the dressing, mix:

1 tablespoon extra virgin olive oil
1 teaspoon balsamic vinegar
Pinch of salt and pepper

SMOKED HAM, FETA, CABBAGE & CHERRY TOMATOES

For the salad, assemble:

Generous 1 cup shredded sweetheart or napa cabbage
⅔ cup cherry tomatoes, quartered
Generous ⅓ cup chopped cucumber
Generous ¼ cup cubed feta
2 ounces smoked ham, sliced
Bunch of fresh chives, chopped
A few fresh flat-leaf parsley leaves

For the dressing, mix:

1 tablespoon extra virgin olive oil
1 teaspoon cider vinegar
Pinch of salt and pepper

VEGAN ALTERNATIVE
Add 3½ ounces edamame, or canned black-eyed peas or chickpeas

KALE, RED PEPPER & CUCUMBER

For the salad, assemble:

2 to 3 leaves of kale, shredded (discard the stems)
3½ ounces cucumber, cut into thin sticks
½ small Italian sweet red pepper, sliced
Handful of pine nuts
Handful of fresh cilantro leaves

For the dressing, mix:

2 teaspoons sweet white miso
1 tablespoon peanut oil
1 teaspoon cider vinegar
Pinch of salt and pepper
1 teaspoon agave nectar
¾-inch fresh ginger, peeled and grated

VEGAN

VEGETARIAN ALTERNATIVE

Replace the plain soy yogurt with plain yogurt or heavy cream

QUINOA, CHICKPEAS & ROASTED EGGPLANT

For the salad, assemble:

Generous ¾ cup cooked red and white quinoa
⅔ cup canned chickpeas
½ chopped and roasted eggplant
Handful of fresh flat-leaf parsley leaves

For the dressing, mix:

1 tablespoon extra virgin olive oil
1 teaspoon cider vinegar
Pinch of salt
1 teaspoon tahini
1 tablespoon plain soy yogurt
2 pinches of saffron threads

TUNA, CHICKPEAS & CHERRY TOMATOES

For the salad, assemble:

⅔ cup cherry tomatoes, quartered
⅔ cup canned chickpeas
½ head of Boston lettuce
*3½ ounces canned tuna (preserved in water),
    flaked*
Bunch of fresh chives, chopped

For the dressing, mix:

1 tablespoon extra virgin olive oil
1 teaspoon lemon juice
Pinch of salt and pepper

FALL

BLACK BEANS, AVOCADO & BROWN RICE

For the salad, assemble:

½ cup cooked brown basmati rice
⅔ cup canned black beans
½ avocado, chopped
Handful of cherry tomatoes, quartered
Handful of fresh cilantro leaves
1 small red chile, minced

For the dressing, mix:

1 tablespoon extra virgin olive oil
1 teaspoon lemon juice
Pinch of salt and pepper

OAK-SMOKED CHEDDAR, PLUMS & RASPBERRIES

For the salad, assemble:

2 ounces baby spinach
2 yellow plums, chopped
Generous ¾ cup raspberries
Generous ¼ cup chopped oak-smoked
  Cheddar cheese
Handful of pine nuts
Handful of fresh mint leaves

For the dressing, mix:

1 tablespoon extra virgin olive oil
1 teaspoon balsamic vinegar
Pinch of salt and pepper

RAW ALTERNATIVE

Replace the hot-smoked salmon with 1 avocado and ½ small red chile, and use freshly shucked corn

HOT-SMOKED SALMON, CORN & BROCCOLI

For the salad, assemble:

2 ounces arugula
Generous ½ cup fresh or canned corn
3½ ounces broccoli, chopped
2 ounces hot-smoked salmon, flaked
Bunch of fresh chives, chopped

For the dressing, mix:

1 tablespoon extra virgin olive oil
1 teaspoon balsamic vinegar
Pinch of salt and pepper

SMOKED HAM, COUSCOUS, BROCCOLI & PEAS

For the salad, assemble:

Scant ⅔ cup cooked whole-wheat couscous
Scant ⅓ cup steamed peas
3½ ounces broccoli, chopped
2 ounces smoked ham, sliced
Bunch of fresh chives, chopped

For the dressing, mix:

1 tablespoon extra virgin olive oil
1 teaspoon cider vinegar
Pinch of salt and pepper
Pinch of dried parsley

PESCATARIAN ALTERNATIVE

Add 2 ounces cooked fish or seafood (e.g., tuna, anchovies, salmon, or shrimp)

BROCCOLI, CORN & CHERRY TOMATOES

For the salad, assemble:

2¼ ounces red oakleaf lettuce
⅓ cup cherry tomatoes, halved
3½ ounces broccoli, chopped
Handful of freshly shucked corn
Handful of fresh flat-leaf parsley leaves
2 scallions, chopped

For the dressing, mix:

1 tablespoon extra virgin olive oil
1 teaspoon cider vinegar
Pinch of salt and pepper

VEGAN

VEGETARIAN ALTERNATIVE

Add some Parmesan or pecorino shavings

CANNELLINI BEANS, TOMATOES & HUMMUS

For the salad, assemble:

2 ounces mixed salad greens
1 cup cherry tomatoes, halved
1 cup canned cannellini beans

For the dressing, mix:

1 tablespoon extra virgin olive oil
1 teaspoon cider vinegar
1 tablespoon hummus
Pinch of salt and pepper

RAW
ALTERNATIVE
*Replace the chicken
with snow peas or sugar
snap peas, and the
quinoa with
baby corn*

ROASTED CHICKEN, QUINOA, RED PEPPER & PEANUTS

For the salad, assemble:

½ cup cooked red and white quinoa
½ small Italian sweet red pepper, sliced
Handful of bean sprouts
2 ounces roasted chicken, sliced
Handful of peanuts
2 scallions, thinly sliced
Handful of fresh cilantro leaves

For the dressing, mix:

1 tablespoon vegetable oil
1 teaspoon lime juice
Pinch of salt
Pinch of chili powder
1 teaspoon agave nectar

SMOKED MACKEREL, QUINOA & ZUCCHINI

For the salad, assemble:

*1 small zucchini, shaved into ribbons with
   a vegetable peeler*
⅔ cup red and yellow cherry tomatoes, halved
Generous ¼ cup cooked black quinoa
2 ounces smoked mackerel, flaked
Handful of fresh flat-leaf parsley leaves

For the dressing, mix:

1 tablespoon extra virgin olive oil
1 teaspoon lemon juice
Pinch of salt and pepper

SHIITAKE MUSHROOMS, RED PEPPER & NORI

For the salad, assemble:

2 ounces arugula

½ red bell pepper, sliced

Scant 1½ cups sliced and fried shiitake mushrooms

*Handful of shredded and toasted nori (toasted
seaweed), tossed with a dash of sunflower oil and
soy sauce*

1 teaspoon toasted sesame seeds

2 scallions, thinly sliced

For the dressing, mix:

1 tablespoon vegetable oil

1 teaspoon toasted sesame oil

1 teaspoon tamari soy sauce

Pinch of salt and pepper

TUNA, ZUCCHINI, BROCCOLI & BLACK OLIVES

For the salad, assemble:

2 ounces baby spinach
*½ zucchini, shaved into ribbons with
  a vegetable peeler*
2 ounces broccoli, chopped
2 ounces canned tuna (preserved in water), flaked
Handful of pitted black olives
Bunch of fresh chives, chopped

For the dressing, mix:

1 tablespoon extra virgin olive oil
1 teaspoon cider vinegar
Pinch of salt and pepper

OMNIVORE ALTERNATIVE

Add 2 ounces roast beef or smoked ham

BROCCOLI, CARROT & CHERRY TOMATOES

For the salad, assemble:

1 purple (or regular) carrot, shaved into ribbons with a vegetable peeler

3½ ounces broccoli, chopped

⅔ cup cherry tomatoes, quartered

Handful of capers

2 tablespoons pumpkin seeds

2 tablespoons shelled hemp seeds

For the dressing, mix:

1 tablespoon extra virgin olive oil

1 teaspoon cider vinegar

Pinch of salt and pepper

GREEN BEANS, NEW POTATOES & BROCCOLI

For the salad, assemble:

4 to 5 halved steamed new potatoes
2 ounces steamed green beans
2 ounces steamed broccoli
Handful of pine nuts
Sprinkle of fresh thyme leaves

For the dressing, mix:

1 tablespoon extra virgin olive oil
1 teaspoon cider vinegar
1 tablespoon vegan cream (e.g., soy or coconut)
Pinch of salt and pepper

FENNEL, BLUE CHEESE & PISTACHIOS

For the salad, assemble:

2¼ ounces romaine lettuce, shredded
½ fennel, thinly sliced
½ cup crumbled blue cheese
Handful of toasted pistachios

For the dressing, mix:

1 tablespoon extra virgin olive oil
1 teaspoon balsamic vinegar
Pinch of salt and pepper
1 tablespoon fennel seeds

FETA, RED PEPPER, CELERY & ALMONDS

For the salad, assemble:

2 celery stalks, sliced
1 red bell pepper, sliced
Generous ¼ cup cubed feta
Handful of almonds, chopped
Handful of raisins
Pinch of dried red pepper flakes

For the dressing, mix:

1 tablespoon extra virgin olive oil
1 teaspoon balsamic vinegar
Pinch of salt and pepper

VEGAN

PESCATARIAN
ALTERNATIVE
*Add some roasted
salmon or cooked shrimp*

QUINOA, FRIED ZUCCHINI & ARUGULA

For the salad, assemble:

2 ounces arugula
½ cup cooked red and white quinoa
1 chopped and fried zucchini
Bunch of fresh basil leaves

For the dressing, mix:

1 tablespoon extra virgin olive oil
1 teaspoon balsamic vinegar
Pinch of salt and pepper

QUINOA, SUGAR SNAP PEAS, BROCCOLI & MUSHROOMS

For the salad, assemble:

½ cup cooked red and white quinoa
Handful of sugar snap peas
3½ ounces broccoli, chopped
¾ cup sliced white mushrooms
1 cup Parmesan cheese shavings
Handful of walnuts, chopped
Handful of fresh flat-leaf parsley leaves

For the dressing, mix:

1 tablespoon extra virgin olive oil
1 teaspoon balsamic vinegar
Pinch of salt and pepper

ROAST BEEF, CARROT & BABY CHARD

For the salad, assemble:

2 ounces baby chard
1 carrot, shredded with a julienne peeler
2 ounces roast beef, thinly sliced
1 cup pecorino shavings
Handful of fresh chives, chopped

For the dressing, mix:

1 tablespoon extra virgin olive oil
1 teaspoon balsamic vinegar
Pinch of salt and pepper

SHRIMP, RED RICE, CUCUMBER & NORI

For the salad, assemble:

3½ ounces cucumber, cut into long thin sticks
½ cup cooked red rice
2 ounces cooked shrimp
2 scallions, sliced
1 teaspoon nori (toasted seaweed) sprinkle
1 teaspoon poppy seeds

For the dressing, mix:

1 tablespoon extra virgin olive oil
1 teaspoon light soy sauce
1 teaspoon wasabi powder
¾–inch fresh ginger, peeled and grated
1 teaspoon toasted sesame oil

VEGAN
ALTERNATIVE
*Replace the almonds in
the dressing with coconut
cream*

KALE, RASPBERRIES & BLACKBERRIES

For the salad, assemble:

*Generous 1 cup shredded kale
  (discard the stems)
Handful of raspberries
Handful of blackberries*

For the dressing, blend together:

*1 tablespoon extra virgin olive oil
Handful of almonds, soaked in water overnight
  then drained
1 tablespoon water
1 teaspoon lemon juice
Pinch of salt*

ROASTED EGGPLANT, CHICKPEAS & POMEGRANATE

For the salad, assemble:

1 small cucumber, cut into long thin sticks
2/3 cup canned chickpeas
Handful of pomegranate seeds
1 eggplant, cubed and roasted
Handful of fresh mint leaves

For the dressing, mix:

1 tablespoon extra virgin olive oil
2 tablespoons plain soy yogurt
Pinch of salt and pepper

OMNIVORE

RAW
ALTERNATIVE
*Replace the coppa ham
with the other half of
the pear*

COPPA HAM, PEAR, BLACKBERRIES & WALNUTS

For the salad, assemble:

2 ounces mixed salad greens
Handful of blackberries
½ pear, chopped
Handful of pomegranate seeds
2 ounces coppa ham, thinly sliced
Handful of walnuts

For the dressing, mix:

1 tablespoon extra virgin olive oil
1 teaspoon balsamic vinegar
Pinch of salt and pepper

VEGETARIAN

VEGAN
ALTERNATIVE
*Replace the cottage
cheese with melon*

BLACKBERRIES, COTTAGE CHEESE, SPINACH & CROUTONS

For the salad, assemble:

2 ounces baby spinach
Scant ¾ cup blackberries
Handful of whole-wheat croutons
Scant ½ cup cottage cheese
Bunch of fresh chives, chopped

For the dressing, mix:

1 tablespoon extra virgin olive oil
1 teaspoon balsamic vinegar
Pinch of salt and pepper

ROASTED EGGPLANT, TOMATOES & PESTO

For the salad, assemble:

2¼ ounces red oakleaf lettuce (or mixed salad greens)
½ cup chopped tomatoes
1 eggplant, cubed and roasted
Handful of fresh basil leaves

For the dressing, mix:

1 tablespoon extra virgin olive oil
1 tablespoon Raw Green Pesto (page 25)
Pinch of salt and pepper

VEGETARIAN ALTERNATIVE
Add 2 ounces firm goat cheese, Brie, or blue cheese, such as Stilton

CARROT, MUSHROOMS, POMEGRANATE & WALNUTS

For the salad, assemble:

2¼ ounces mixed salad greens
1 purple (or regular) carrot, shaved into ribbons
with a vegetable peeler
Scant 1½ cups sliced brown mushrooms
Handful of pomegranate seeds
Handful of walnuts, chopped
Handful of fresh flat-leaf parsley leaves

For the dressing, mix:

1 tablespoon extra virgin olive oil
1 teaspoon cider vinegar
Pinch of salt and pepper
2 tablespoons Nut & Lemon dressing
(page 26, made with walnuts)

RED PEPPER, CARROT & CASHEWS

For the salad, assemble:

1 carrot, shaved into ribbons with a vegetable peeler
1 Italian sweet red pepper, sliced
2 scallions, thinly sliced
Handful of cashews
Handful of fresh cilantro leaves

For the dressing, blend together:

2 tablespoons coconut water
2 tablespoons cashews
1 tablespoon vegetable oil
1 teaspoon lemon juice
¾–inch fresh ginger, peeled and grated

FETA, YELLOW PEPPER, SPINACH & BLACK OLIVES

For the salad, assemble:

2 ounces baby spinach
1 yellow bell pepper, sliced
½ small red onion, thinly sliced
Generous ¼ cup cubed feta
Handful of pitted black olives, halved

For the dressing, mix:

1 tablespoon extra virgin olive oil
1 teaspoon cider vinegar
Pinch of salt and pepper

VEGETARIAN
ALTERNATIVE
*Replace the anchovies
with goat cheese or feta*

ANCHOVIES, CAULIFLOWER, CAPERS & TOMATOES

For the salad, assemble:

3½ ounces cauliflower, finely chopped
Scant ½ cup cherry tomatoes, chopped
Handful of capers
2 ounces marinated anchovies, chopped
Handful of fresh flat-leaf parsley leaves
Bunch of fresh chives, chopped

For the dressing, mix:

1 tablespoon extra virgin olive oil
1 teaspoon balsamic vinegar
Pinch of salt
Pinch of red pepper

FETA, COUSCOUS & ROASTED EGGPLANT

For the salad, assemble:

Scant ²/₃ cup cooked whole-wheat couscous
¹/₂ cubed and roasted eggplant
Handful of sun-dried tomatoes
Generous ¹/₄ cup cubed feta
Handful of fresh mint leaves

For the dressing, mix:

1 tablespoon extra virgin olive oil
1 teaspoon balsamic vinegar
Pinch of salt and pepper

VEGAN
ALTERNATIVE

*Add ⅔ cup canned
chickpeas or steamed
green beans*

BEET, ZUCCHINI, POMEGRANATE & ALFALFA

For the salad, assemble:

*2 ounces mixed salad greens (e.g., watercress, arugula,
    chard, and red oakleaf lettuce)*
1 small beet, diced
1 zucchini, cut into thin sticks
Handful of pomegranate seeds
1 tablespoon shelled hemp seeds
Handful of alfalfa sprouts

For the dressing, mix:

1 tablespoon extra virgin olive oil
1 teaspoon cider vinegar
Pinch of salt and pepper
*1 tablespoon raw mustard (made from soaking
    2 tablespoons yellow mustard seeds,
    2 tablespoons brown mustard seeds,
    2 tablespoons cider vinegar, 1 tablespoon water,
    and 1 teaspoon agave nectar together overnight,
    and then blending until smooth)*

ROAST BEEF, BEET, POMEGRANATE & ORANGE ZEST

For the salad, assemble:

2 ounces baby spinach
½ beet, thinly sliced
Handful of pomegranate seeds
3½ ounces roast beef, thinly sliced
*Sprinkle of orange zest, removed with
  a vegetable peeler*
Handful of walnuts, chopped
Sprinkle of fresh thyme leaves

For the dressing, mix:

1 tablespoon extra virgin olive oil
1 teaspoon orange juice
Pinch of salt and pepper

PECORINO, SUN-DRIED TOMATOES & GREEN BEANS

For the salad, assemble:

3½ ounces steamed green beans
Handful of sun-dried tomatoes, sliced
1 cup pecorino shavings
2 scallions, thinly sliced
Handful of fresh flat-leaf parsley leaves

For the dressing, mix:

1 tablespoon extra virgin olive oil
1 teaspoon balsamic vinegar
Pinch of salt and pepper

PESCATARIAN

VEGAN ALTERNATIVE

Replace the tuna with a handful of black olives

TUNA, COUSCOUS, GREEN BEANS & CHERRY TOMATOES

For the salad, assemble:

Scant ⅔ cup cooked couscous
3½ ounces steamed green beans
⅔ cup cherry tomatoes, halved
2 ounces canned tuna (preserved in water), flaked
Handful of fresh flat-leaf parsley leaves

For the dressing, mix:

1 tablespoon extra virgin olive oil
1 teaspoon lemon juice
Pinch of salt and pepper

VEGAN

PESCATARIAN ALTERNATIVE
Add some marinated anchovies or smoked mackerel

LIMA BEANS, ZUCCHINI & BLACK OLIVES

For the salad, assemble:

1 head of Boston lettuce
1 zucchini, shredded with a julienne peeler
⅔ cup canned lima beans
Handful of fresh basil leaves
Handful of pitted black olives, halved

For the dressing, mix:

1 teaspoon extra virgin olive oil
1 tablespoon Olive Tapenade (page 25)
1 teaspoon cider vinegar
Pinch of salt and pepper

VEGAN ALTERNATIVE
Add 2 ounces steamed green beans or peas, or some cooked red quinoa

SUN-DRIED TOMATOES, ZUCCHINI & PINE NUTS

For the salad, assemble:

*2 small zucchini, shaved into ribbons with
   a vegetable peeler*
Handful of sun-dried tomatoes
Handful of raw pitted black olives, halved
Handful of pine nuts
Handful of fresh dill fronds

For the dressing, mix:

1 tablespoon extra virgin olive oil
1 teaspoon cider vinegar
Pinch of salt and pepper

RAW

VEGETARIAN ALTERNATIVE

Add some medium-hard cheese, such as Manchego, Gouda, or Cheddar

KALE, AVOCADO & SPROUTED BEANS

For the salad, assemble:

Generous 1 cup shredded kale (discard the stems)
⅔ cup cherry tomatoes, halved
¼ small red onion, minced
1 avocado, chopped
Handful of sprouted beans

For the dressing, mix:

1 tablespoon extra virgin olive oil
1 teaspoon cider vinegar
Pinch of salt and pepper

TUNA, KALE, CARROT & SUN-DRIED TOMATOES

For the salad, assemble:

½ cup shredded kale (discard the stems)
½ small carrot, shaved into ribbons with a vegetable peeler
Handful of sun-dried tomatoes
2 ounces canned tuna (preserved in water), flaked
Handful of pine nuts
Bunch of fresh chives, chopped

For the dressing, mix:

1 tablespoon extra virgin olive oil
1 teaspoon lemon juice
Pinch of salt and pepper

SPECK, BLUE CHEESE, BLACKBERRIES & CELERY

For the salad, assemble:

2 ounces mixed salad greens
Handful of blackberries
1 celery stalk, sliced
2 ounces speck ham, thinly sliced
½ cup crumbled blue cheese
Handful of walnuts, chopped
Handful of fresh mint leaves

For the dressing, mix:

1 tablespoon extra virgin olive oil
1 teaspoon balsamic vinegar
Pinch of salt and pepper

RAW

VEGETARIAN
ALTERNATIVE
*Add cheese, such as
salted ricotta, goat cheese,
or young pecorino*

FIGS, BLACKBERRIES & HAZELNUTS

For the salad, assemble:

*2 ounces mixed salad greens (e.g., chard, watercress,
and red oakleaf lettuce)*
Handful of blackberries
2 figs, cut into wedges
Handful of hazelnuts, chopped
Handful of fresh mint leaves

For the dressing, mix:

1 tablespoon extra virgin olive oil
1 teaspoon cider vinegar
Pinch of salt and pepper

PECORINO, BLACK GRAPES & PINE NUTS

For the salad, assemble:

*3¹/₂ ounces mixed baby salad greens (e.g., watercress,
    chard, and red oakleaf lettuce)*
Scant ³/₄ cup black grapes, halved
1 cup pecorino shavings
Handful of pine nuts

For the dressing, mix:

1 tablespoon extra virgin olive oil
1 teaspoon balsamic vinegar
Pinch of salt and pepper

VEGETARIAN
ALTERNATIVE
Replace the Nut &
Lemon dressing with light
cream or plain yogurt

RED GRAPES, CELERY & WALNUTS

For the salad, assemble:

2 ounces arugula
Handful of red grapes, halved
2 celery stalks, sliced
Handful of walnuts, chopped
Handful of fresh flat-leaf parsley leaves

For the dressing, mix:

1 tablespoon extra virgin olive oil
1 teaspoon lemon juice
Pinch of salt and pepper
2 tablespoons Nut & Lemon dressing
   (page 26, made with walnuts)

SHRIMP, ZUCCHINI, CARROT & PINE NUTS

For the salad, assemble:

*½ small zucchini, shaved into ribbons with
  a vegetable peeler*
*½ small purple (or regular) carrot, shaved into
  ribbons with a vegetable peeler*
1 ounce arugula
2 ounces cooked shrimp
Handful of pine nuts
Bunch of fresh chives, chopped

For the dressing, mix:

1 tablespoon extra virgin olive oil
1 tablespoon mayonnaise
1 teaspoon cider vinegar
Pinch of salt and pepper
1 teaspoon smoked paprika

CANNELLINI BEANS, ZUCCHINI & PESTO

For the salad, assemble:

1 zucchini, shredded with a julienne peeler
²/₃ cup canned cannellini beans
2 scallions, thinly sliced
Handful of pine nuts
Handful of fresh basil leaves

For the dressing, mix:

1 tablespoon extra virgin olive oil
1 teaspoon balsamic vinegar
Pinch of salt and pepper
2 tablespoons Raw Green Pesto (page 25)

143

VEGETARIAN ALTERNATIVE

Replace the chicken with canned cannellini beans or lentils

ROASTED CHICKEN, ZUCCHINI, CABBAGE & MANCHEGO

For the salad, assemble:

Generous 1 cup finely shredded green or savoy cabbage

1 zucchini, cubed and roasted

2 ounces roasted chicken, sliced

Generous ¼ cup cubed Manchego (or Gouda or Cheddar cheese)

Handful of fresh lemon thyme leaves

For the dressing, mix:

1 tablespoon extra virgin olive oil

1 teaspoon balsamic vinegar

Pinch of salt and pepper

VEGETARIAN

OMNIVORE ALTERNATIVE

Add 2 ounces spicy roasted chicken

GOUDA, BLACK BEANS, CORN & SUN-DRIED TOMATOES

For the salad, assemble:

2 ounces salad greens (e.g., frisée and mâche)
⅔ cup canned black beans
Handful of fresh or canned corn
Handful of sun-dried tomatoes, sliced
Generous ¼ cup cubed Gouda (or Manchego or Cheddar cheese)
Handful of fresh cilantro leaves

For the dressing, mix:

1 tablespoon chili-infused extra virgin olive oil
1 teaspoon balsamic vinegar
Pinch of salt and pepper

VEGAN ALTERNATIVE
Replace the anchovies with a handful each of capers and black olives

ANCHOVIES, COUSCOUS, CUCUMBER & LEMON ZEST

For the salad, assemble:

Scant ⅔ cup cooked pearl couscous
3½ ounces cucumber, chopped
2 ounces marinated anchovies, chopped
Sprinkle of lemon zest, removed with a
   vegetable peeler
Handful of fresh flat-leaf parsley leaves

For the dressing, mix:

1 tablespoon extra virgin olive oil
1 teaspoon lemon juice
Pinch of salt and pepper
Pinch of dried red pepper flakes

GLUTEN-FREE PASTA, BLACK OLIVES & CHILE

For the salad, assemble:

3¹/₂ ounces cooked gluten-free penne
²/₃ cup cherry tomatoes, halved
2 scallions, thinly sliced
Handful of pitted black olives, chopped
Handful of fresh flat-leaf parsley leaves
1 small red chile, seeded and thinly sliced

For the dressing, mix:

1 tablespoon extra virgin olive oil
Pinch of salt and pepper

OMNIVORE
ALTERNATIVE
*Add 2 ounces roast beef
or smoked ham*

RED CABBAGE, YELLOW TOMATOES & RED PEPPER

For the salad, assemble:

Generous 1 cup finely shredded red cabbage
1 red bell pepper, thinly sliced
½ cup chopped yellow tomatoes
1 teaspoon pumpkin seeds
Sprinkle of fresh thyme leaves

For the dressing, mix:

1 tablespoon extra virgin olive oil
1 teaspoon cider vinegar
Pinch of salt and pepper

PROSCIUTTO, MANGO, TARRAGON & SESAME SEEDS

For the salad, assemble:

3¼ ounces mixed salad greens (e.g., watercress and
   wild arugula)
3½ ounces mango, sliced
2 scallions, thinly sliced
2 ounces prosciutto, thinly sliced
1 tablespoon sesame seeds
Handful of fresh tarragon leaves

For the dressing, mix:

1 tablespoon extra virgin olive oil
1 teaspoon balsamic vinegar
Pinch of salt and pepper

SCAMORZA, SPELT, ARTICHOKES & CARROT

For the salad, assemble:

Scant ⅔ cup cooked spelt

*1 small carrot, shaved into ribbons with a
vegetable peeler*

*Handful of grilled, marinated artichoke hearts,
chopped*

¼ cup cubed scamorza (smoked cheese)

1 tablespoon sesame seeds

Handful of fresh flat-leaf parsley leaves

For the dressing, mix:

1 tablespoon extra virgin olive oil

1 teaspoon balsamic vinegar

Pinch of salt and pepper

SMOKED MACKEREL, COUSCOUS & ROASTED BEET

For the salad, assemble:

Scant ⅔ cup cooked whole-wheat couscous
1 roasted beet, chopped
2 ounces broccoli, chopped
2 ounces smoked mackerel, flaked
1 tablespoon mustard seeds
Handful of fresh flat-leaf parsley leaves

For the dressing, mix:

1 tablespoon extra virgin olive oil
1 teaspoon lemon juice
Pinch of salt and pepper

BRESAOLA, QUINOA, CORN & BROCCOLI

For the salad, assemble:

½ cup cooked white quinoa
2 ounces broccoli, chopped
⅓ cup cherry tomatoes, halved
Generous ¼ cup fresh or canned corn
1 scallion, thinly sliced
2 ounces bresaola (air-dried beef), thinly sliced
Handful of fresh flat-leaf parsley leaves

For the dressing, mix:

1 tablespoon extra virgin olive oil
1 teaspoon cider vinegar
Pinch of salt and pepper

FENNEL, BROCCOLI, POMEGRANATE & HUMMUS

For the salad, assemble:

2 ounces arugula

2 ounces broccoli, chopped

½ small fennel bulb, thinly sliced

Handful of pomegranate seeds

2 scallions, sliced

1 tablespoon sesame seeds

Handful of fresh mint leaves

For the dressing, mix:

1 tablespoon extra virgin olive oil

1 teaspoon cider vinegar

1 tablespoon hummus

Pinch of salt and pepper

Pinch of smoked paprika

VEGETARIAN ALTERNATIVE

Replace the Nut & Lemon dressing with plain yogurt

FIGS, FENNEL & POMEGRANATE

For the salad, assemble:

2 ounces arugula
1 small fennel bulb, thinly sliced
2 figs, quartered
Handful of pomegranate seeds
Bunch of fresh chives, chopped

For the dressing, mix:

1 tablespoon extra virgin olive oil
1 teaspoon lemon juice
Pinch of salt and pepper
2 tablespoons Nut & Lemon dressing
(page 26, made with cashews)

FIGS, GOAT CHEESE & WALNUTS

For the salad, assemble:

2 ounces baby spinach
2 figs, quartered
Generous ¼ cup chopped firm goat cheese
Handful of walnuts
Handful of fresh mint leaves

For the dressing, mix:

1 tablespoon extra virgin olive oil
1 teaspoon balsamic vinegar
Pinch of salt and pepper

KALE, GREEN BEANS & CHERRY TOMATOES

For the salad, assemble:

¾ cup finely chopped kale (discard the stems)
Handful of cherry tomatoes, quartered
Handful of green beans or sugar snap peas
1 tablespoon sesame seeds
Handful of fresh mint leaves

For the dressing, mix:

1 tablespoon extra virgin olive oil
1 teaspoon cider vinegar
2 tablespoons Raw Nut & Agave dressing
    (page 27, made with sesame seeds instead
    of cashews)
Pinch of salt and pepper

PESCATARIAN

RAW
ALTERNATIVE
*Replace the mackerel
with a handful of
radishes*

SMOKED MACKEREL, BROCCOLI & CHERRY TOMATOES

For the salad, assemble:

2 ounces watercress
3½ ounces broccoli, chopped
*Handful of yellow and red cherry tomatoes,
   halved*
2 ounces smoked mackerel, flaked
Handful of pine nuts
Handful of fresh flat-leaf parsley leaves

For the dressing, mix:

1 tablespoon extra virgin olive oil
1 teaspoon lemon juice
Pinch of salt and pepper

VEGETARIAN

PESCATARIAN
ALTERNATIVE
*Replace the Parmesan
with smoked salmon*

QUAIL EGGS, PARMESAN, FENNEL & SUN-DRIED TOMATOES

For the salad, assemble:

2 ounces arugula
½ fennel bulb, thinly sliced
Handful of sun-dried tomatoes, chopped
3 to 4 hard-boiled quail eggs, halved
1 cup Parmesan cheese shavings
Handful of pine nuts
Handful of fresh flat-leaf parsley leaves

For the dressing, mix:

1 tablespoon extra virgin olive oil
1 teaspoon cider vinegar
Pinch of salt and pepper

PURPLE POTATOES, PEAS & CARROT

For the salad, assemble:

*1 carrot, shaved into ribbons with a
 vegetable peeler*
Scant ⅓ cup fresh or steamed peas
*3½ ounces chopped and steamed purple
 (or regular) new potatoes*
Handful of fresh flat-leaf parsley leaves

For the dressing, mix:

1 teaspoon extra virgin olive oil
*1 tablespoon vegan cream (e.g., soy yogurt
 or coconut cream)*
1 teaspoon cider vinegar
Pinch of salt
Pinch of saffron threads

OMNIVORE

VEGAN ALTERNATIVE
Replace the chicken with ⅔ cup of your favorite canned beans

ROASTED CHICKEN, BLACK QUINOA & MARINATED PEPPERS

For the salad, assemble:

2 ounces arugula
Generous ¼ cup cooked black quinoa
Handful of marinated peppers from a jar
2 ounces roasted chicken, sliced
Handful of fresh cilantro leaves

For the dressing, mix:

1 tablespoon extra virgin olive oil
1 teaspoon balsamic vinegar
Pinch of salt and pepper

VEGAN

VEGETARIAN ALTERNATIVE
Add 2 ounces pecorino

ROASTED VEGETABLES, COUSCOUS & BLACK OLIVES

For the salad, assemble:

Scant ⅔ cup cooked pearl couscous
½ yellow bell pepper, cubed and roasted
½ red bell pepper, cubed and roasted
1 small zucchini, cubed and roasted
1 small red onion, cubed and roasted
2 ounces arugula
Handful of pitted black olives, halved

For the dressing, mix:

1 tablespoon extra virgin olive oil
1 teaspoon balsamic vinegar
Pinch of salt and pepper

SQUID, BROCCOLI & AVOCADO

For the salad, assemble:

*2 ounces watercress
2 ounces broccoli, chopped
1 avocado, chopped
2 ounces broiled squid, sliced
Handful of pumpkin seeds
Bunch of fresh chives, chopped*

For the dressing, mix:

*1 tablespoon extra virgin olive oil
1 teaspoon lemon juice
Pinch of salt and pepper
Pinch of dried red pepper flakes*

PASTRAMI, BROWN RICE & ROASTED ZUCCHINI

For the salad, assemble:

¼ cup cooked brown short-grain rice

3½ ounces cucumber, shredded with a julienne
  peeler (discard the soft core)

1 small zucchini, cubed and roasted

2 ounces pastrami or roast beef, thinly sliced

Handful of fresh mint leaves

For the dressing, mix:

1 tablespoon extra virgin olive oil

1 teaspoon balsamic vinegar

Pinch of salt and pepper

ROASTED CHICKEN, SPELT & BROCCOLI

For the salad, assemble:

²/₃ cup cooked spelt
3½ ounces raw or steamed broccoli, chopped
²/₃ cup cherry tomatoes, chopped
2 ounces roasted chicken, sliced
2 scallions, thinly sliced
Handful of fresh flat-leaf parsley leaves

For the dressing, mix:

1 tablespoon extra virgin olive oil
1 teaspoon balsamic vinegar
Pinch of salt and pepper

VEGAN

VEGETARIAN ALTERNATIVE
Add 2 ounces goat cheese or blue cheese

ARTICHOKES, LIMA BEANS, CELERY & WALNUTS

For the salad, assemble:

2 celery stalks, sliced
⅔ cup canned lima beans
Handful of grilled, marinated artichoke hearts, chopped
Handful of walnuts, chopped
Bunch of fresh chives, chopped

For the dressing, mix:

1 tablespoon extra virgin olive oil
1 teaspoon balsamic vinegar
Pinch of salt and pepper

VEGETARIAN
ALTERNATIVE
Replace the speck with more sun-dried tomatoes

SPECK, SCAMORZA, SUN-DRIED TOMATOES & RADICCHIO

For the salad, assemble:

2½ ounces radicchio

*Generous ¼ cup finely chopped scamorza
(smoked cheese)*

2 ounces speck ham, roughly shredded

Handful of sun-dried tomatoes, chopped

For the dressing, mix:

1 tablespoon extra virgin olive oil

1 teaspoon balsamic vinegar

Pinch of salt and pepper

MANCHEGO, DRIED APRICOTS, FENNEL & RADICCHIO

For the salad, assemble:

3½ ounces radicchio, shredded
½ fennel bulb, thinly sliced
Handful of dried apricots, chopped
Generous ¼ cup cubed Manchego (or Asiago
   or Gouda cheese)
Handful of almonds
Handful of fresh mint leaves

For the dressing, mix:

1 tablespoon extra virgin olive oil
1 teaspoon cider vinegar
Pinch of salt and pepper

VEGAN
ALTERNATIVE
*Replace the salmon and
caviar with ⅔ cup canned
chickpeas, seasoned with
a pinch of paprika*

SASHIMI SALMON, CAVIAR, PARSNIP & RADICCHIO

For the salad, assemble:

2 ounces radicchio, shredded

*1 small parsnip, shaved into ribbons with
a vegetable peeler*

2 ounces sashimi salmon, thinly sliced

1 teaspoon lumpfish caviar

1 teaspoon toasted sesame seeds

Bunch of fresh chives, chopped

For the dressing, mix:

1 tablespoon extra virgin olive oil

1 teaspoon lemon juice

Pinch of salt

BLACK LENTILS, PARSNIPS & DRIED CRANBERRIES

For the salad, assemble:

Generous 1½ cups cooked black lentils
2 parsnips, shaved into ribbons with
  a vegetable peeler
Handful of dried cranberries
Handful of pine nuts
Bunch of fresh chives, chopped

For the dressing, mix:

1 tablespoon extra virgin olive oil
1 teaspoon balsamic vinegar
Pinch of salt and pepper

VEGETARIAN ALTERNATIVE
Add 2 ounces goat or blue cheese, or pecorino

PEAR, CAULIFLOWER, KALE & PISTACHIOS

For the salad, assemble:

¾ cup chopped kale (discard the stems)
1 pear, chopped
3½ ounces cauliflower, chopped
Bunch of fresh chives, chopped
Handful of pistachios

For the dressing, mix:

1 tablespoon extra virgin olive oil
1 teaspoon lemon juice
Pinch of salt

APPLE, CELERY, WALNUTS & POMEGRANATE SEEDS

For the salad, assemble:

2 ounces romaine lettuce
1 apple, chopped
2 celery stalks, sliced
Handful of walnuts, chopped
Handful of pomegranate seeds

For the dressing, mix:

1 tablespoon extra virgin olive oil
1 teaspoon cider vinegar
Pinch of salt and pepper
2 tablespoons plain yogurt

VEGAN

OMNIVORE
ALTERNATIVE
*Add some roasted
chicken breast, or fried
pancetta or chorizo*

BARLEY, MUSHROOMS & GREEN BEANS

For the salad, assemble:

Scant ⅔ cup cooked barley
3½ ounces steamed green beans
Scant 1½ cups sliced cremini mushrooms
Handful of fresh basil leaves

For the dressing, mix:

1 tablespoon extra virgin olive oil
1 teaspoon balsamic vinegar
Pinch of salt and pepper

VEGAN ALTERNATIVE
Replace the squid with 3 1/2 ounces roasted cauliflower

SQUID, SAFFRON, PEAS & PEARL COUSCOUS

For the salad, assemble:

Scant 2/3 cup cooked pearl couscous
1/2 cup steamed peas
2 ounces cooked squid, sliced
Handful of fresh flat-leaf parsley leaves

For the dressing, mix:

1 tablespoon extra virgin olive oil
1 teaspoon cider vinegar
Pinch of salt and pepper
Pinch of saffron threads

RAW

OMNIVORE ALTERNATIVE
Add 2 ounces roasted chicken or smoked ham

DATES, FENNEL & ALMONDS

For the salad, assemble:

1 head of Boston lettuce
1 small fennel, thinly sliced
Handful of dried, pitted dates
Handful of almonds, soaked in water for 10 minutes
Handful of fresh dill fronds

For the dressing, mix:

1 tablespoon extra virgin olive oil
1 teaspoon cider vinegar
Pinch of salt and pepper
Pinch of crushed fennel seeds

GORGONZOLA, CELERY, PISTACHIOS & PURSLANE

For the salad, assemble:

2 ounces winter purslane or watercress
2 celery stalks, sliced
Handful of pistachios
½ cup crumbled aged Gorgonzola or other blue cheese
Handful of fresh flat-leaf parsley leaves

For the dressing, mix:

1 tablespoon extra virgin olive oil
1 teaspoon balsamic vinegar
Pinch of salt and pepper

OMNIVORE

VEGETARIAN ALTERNATIVE

Replace the chicken with 2 ounces goat cheese, blue cheese, or Brie

ROASTED CHICKEN, COUSCOUS, PEAR & DRIED APRICOTS

For the salad, assemble:

Scant ⅔ cup cooked whole-wheat couscous
1 pear, chopped
Handful of dried apricots, chopped
2 ounces roasted chicken, chopped
Handful of almonds, chopped
Handful of fresh thyme leaves

For the dressing, mix:

1 tablespoon extra virgin olive oil
1 teaspoon balsamic vinegar
Pinch of salt and pepper

PECORINO, COUSCOUS, GREEN OLIVES & PICKLED ONIONS

For the salad, assemble:

Scant ⅔ cup cooked whole-wheat couscous
Generous ¼ cup cubed young pecorino
Handful of pickled baby onions
Handful of pitted green olives, halved
Handful of fresh tarragon leaves

For the dressing, mix:

1 tablespoon extra virgin olive oil
1 teaspoon cider vinegar
Pinch of salt and pepper
Pinch of dried red pepper flakes

VEGETARIAN

VEGAN
ALTERNATIVE
*Replace the blue cheese
with your favorite canned
beans, such as cannellini
beans or black-eyed
peas*

QUINOA, BLUE CHEESE, KALE & ARTICHOKES

For the salad, assemble:

½ cup shredded kale (discard the stems)
½ fennel bulb, thinly sliced
Generous ¼ cup cooked red and white quinoa
*Small handful of grilled, marinated artichoke hearts,
  chopped*
Generous ¼ cup chopped blue cheese
Handful of pistachios
Handful of fresh flat-leaf parsley leaves

For the dressing, mix:

1 tablepsoon extra virgin olive oil
1 teaspoon cider vinegar
Pinch of salt and pepper

CHORIZO, ROASTED POTATOES & RED ONIONS

For the salad, assemble:

⅔ cup shredded kale (discard the stems)
3½ ounces chopped and roasted new potatoes
½ small red onion, thinly sliced
2 ounces chorizo, finely chopped

For the dressing, mix:

1 tablespoon extra virgin olive oil
1 teaspoon cider vinegar
Pinch of salt and pepper
Pinch of smoked paprika

VEGAN

VEGETARIAN ALTERNATIVE

Add 2 ounces firm goat cheese, Parmesan, or pecorino

CANNELLINI BEANS, MUSHROOMS & TRUFFLE CREAM

For the salad, assemble:

2 ounces watercress
Scant 1½ cups sliced cremini mushrooms
⅔ cup canned cannellini beans
Handful of walnuts, chopped

For the dressing, mix:

1 tablespoon extra virgin olive oil
1 teaspoon balsamic vinegar
1 tablespoon oat cream or puréed silken tofu
1 teaspoon white truffle paste
1 teaspoon ground walnuts

RICE, MUSHROOMS, PARMESAN & WATERCRESS

For the salad, assemble:

½ cup cooked white short-grain rice
Scant 1½ cups sliced cremini mushrooms
1 ounce watercress
2 scallions, sliced
1 cup Parmesan cheese shavings

For the dressing, mix:

1 tablespoon extra virgin olive oil
1 teaspoon balsamic vinegar
Pinch of salt and pepper

RAW

PESCATARIAN
ALTERNATIVE
*Add 2 ounces marinated
anchovies*

BEET, BLOOD ORANGE, RAISINS & RADICCHIO

For the salad, assemble:

3½ ounces radicchio, shredded
1 small Sicilian blood orange, thinly sliced
1 beet, thinly sliced
Handful of golden raisins
Handful of pumpkin seeds
Handful of fresh mint leaves

For the dressing, mix:

1 tablespoon extra virgin olive oil
1 teaspoon cider vinegar
Pinch of salt and pepper

SMOKED MACKEREL, ORANGE, KALE & BLACK OLIVES

For the salad, assemble:

⅔ cup chopped kale (discard the stems)
2 ounces smoked mackerel, flaked
Handful of pitted black olives
1 orange, chopped

For the dressing, mix:

1 tablespoon extra virgin olive oil
1 teaspoon lemon juice
Pinch of salt and pepper

CRABMEAT, BLACK QUINOA, EDAMAME & CARROT

For the salad, assemble:

½ cup cooked black quinoa
2 ounces steamed edamame
1 carrot, shaved into ribbons with a vegetable peeler
2 ounces cooked crabmeat
Handful of fresh cilantro leaves

For the dressing, mix:

1 tablespoon extra virgin olive oil
1 teaspoon cider vinegar
Pinch of salt and pepper
1 to 2 pinches of dried red pepper flakes

FENNEL, CARROT, PISTACHIOS & GOJI BERRIES

For the salad, assemble:

2 ounces mixed baby salad greens (e.g., chard and
  red oakleaf lettuce)
1 small carrot, shredded with a julienne peeler
1 small fennel bulb, thinly sliced
Handful of dried goji berries
Handful of pistachios
Bunch of fresh chives, chopped

For the dressing, mix:

1 tablespoon extra virgin olive oil
1 teaspoon cider vinegar
Pinch of salt and pepper

ROASTED CHICKEN, PARSNIP & RED ONION

For the salad, assemble:

2 ounces arugula
1 chopped and roasted parsnip
2 ounces roasted chicken, sliced
1 sliced and roasted red onion
Handful of pine nuts
Handful of fresh thyme leaves

For the dressing, mix:

1 tablespoon extra virgin olive oil
1 teaspoon balsamic vinegar
Pinch of salt and pepper

VEGAN

VEGETARIAN ALTERNATIVE

Replace the vegan cream with light cream or plain yogurt

CELERY, CHICKPEAS, PUMPKIN SEEDS & MINT

For the salad, assemble:

2 celery stalks, sliced
²⁄₃ cup canned chickpeas
Handful of fresh mint leaves
Handful of pumpkin seeds

For the dressing, blend together:

1 tablespoon extra virgin olive oil
1 teaspoon cider vinegar
1 tablespoon vegan cream (e.g. soy or coconut)
Pinch of salt and pepper

VEGAN ALTERNATIVE
Replace the Taleggio with canned green or black lentils

TALEGGIO, JERUSALEM ARTICHOKES & PINE NUTS

For the salad, assemble:

2 ounces mixed baby salad greens (e.g., chard, watercress, and red oakleaf lettuce)

3½ ounces chopped and roasted Jerusalem artichokes

Generous ¼ cup cubed Taleggio (or firm goat cheese)

Handful of pine nuts

Handful of fresh flat-leaf parsley leaves

For the dressing, mix:

1 tablespoon extra virgin olive oil

1 teaspoon balsamic vinegar

Pinch of salt and pepper

VEGETARIAN ALTERNATIVE

Replace the pastrami with 3½ ounces feta or ricotta salata

PASTRAMI, ROASTED SWEET POTATO & KALE

For the salad, assemble:

⅔ cup shredded kale (discard the stems)
½ roasted sweet potato, cubed
Handful of steamed peas
2 ounces pastrami (or roast beef), thinly sliced
Handful of fresh mint leaves

For the dressing, mix:

1 tablespoon extra virgin olive oil
1 teaspoon balsamic vinegar
Pinch of salt and pepper

191

VEGETARIAN ALTERNATIVE
Add 2 ounces Parmesan, pecorino, or firm goat cheese

ROMANESCO, BEET, APPLE & POMEGRANATE

For the salad, assemble:

$3^{1}/_{2}$ *ounces romanesco, chopped*
1 apple, chopped
$^{1}/_{2}$ *small beet, grated*
Handful of pomegranate seeds
Handful of pumpkin seeds
Handful of fresh flat-leaf parsley leaves

For the dressing, mix:

1 tablespoon extra virgin olive oil
1 teaspoon cider vinegar
Pinch of salt and pepper

PARSNIP, BEET & GOAT CHEESE

For the salad, assemble:

2 ounces watercress

*1 small parsnip, shaved into ribbons with
a vegetable peeler*

½ small beet, cut into thin sticks

Generous ¼ cup chopped firm goat cheese

Handful of pomegranate seeds

Handful of pistachios

Handful of fresh thyme leaves

For the dressing, mix:

1 tablespoon extra virgin olive oil

1 teaspoon balsamic vinegar

Pinch of salt and pepper

VEGAN ALTERNATIVE
Add scant ¼ cup coconut cream or 2 ounces whole-wheat croutons

WHITE GRAPEFRUIT, KALE, APPLE & POMEGRANATE

For the salad, assemble:

½ cup chopped kale (discard the stems)
1 white grapefruit, chopped
1 apple, thinly sliced
Handful of pomegranate seeds
Handful of pumpkin seeds

For the dressing, mix:

1 tablespoon extra virgin olive oil
1 teaspoon cider vinegar
Pinch of salt and pepper

ROASTED CHICKEN, BLACK RICE & ORANGE

For the salad, assemble:

½ cup cooked black rice
1 orange, chopped
2 ounces roasted chicken breast, chopped
Handful of walnuts, chopped
Handful of raisins
Bunch of fresh chives, chopped

For the dressing, mix:

1 tablespoon extra virgin olive oil
1 teaspoon cider vinegar
Pinch of salt and pepper
Orange zest, removed with vegetable peeler

VEGAN

OMNIVORE ALTERNATIVE

Add 2 ounces chorizo or roasted chicken breast

ROASTED BUTTERNUT SQUASH, RED ONIONS, & CHICKPEAS

For the salad, assemble:

2 ounces arugula
½ cup chopped and roasted butternut squash
1 sliced and roasted red onion
⅔ cup canned chickpeas

For the dressing, mix:

1 tablespoon extra virgin olive oil
1 teaspoon balsamic vinegar
Pinch of salt and pepper

VEGAN ALTERNATIVE

Replace the sardines with a handful of sun-dried tomatoes

SARDINES, PINTO BEANS & AVOCADO

For the salad, assemble:

1 heads of Boston lettuce
1 small avocado, chopped
2/3 cup canned pinto beans (or cranberry beans)
2 ounces canned sardines, flaked
2 scallions, sliced

For the dressing, mix:

1 tablespoon extra virgin olive oil
1 teaspoon lemon juice
Pinch of salt and pepper

OMNIVORE

VEGETARIAN ALTERNATIVE
Simply omit the chorizo, or add more Manchego and roasted onion

CHORIZO, CHILI MANCHEGO & ROASTED SWEET POTATO

For the salad, assemble:

1 head of red chicory, shredded
½ roasted sweet potato, chopped
1 sliced and roasted red onion
2 ounces chorizo, cubed
Generous ¼ cup cubed chili manchego (or scamorza smoked cheese)
Handful of fresh flat-leaf parsley leaves

For the dressing, mix:

1 tablespoon extra virgin olive oil
1 teaspoon balsamic vinegar
Pinch of salt and pepper

COUSCOUS, PECORINO, APPLE, PECANS & DATES

For the salad, assemble:

Scant ⅔ cup cooked whole-wheat couscous
1 apple, chopped
Generous ¼ cup cubed young pecorino
  (or smoked Cheddar cheese)
Handful of dried, pitted dates, chopped
Handful of pecans (or walnuts), chopped
1 teaspoon fresh thyme leaves

For the dressing, mix:

1 tablespoon extra virgin olive oil
1 teaspoon lemon juice
Pinch of salt and pepper

RED CABBAGE, MUSHROOMS & CARROT

For the salad, assemble:

Generous 1 cup shredded red cabbage

1 small purple (or regular) carrot, shaved into ribbons
  with a vegetable peeler

Scant 1½ cups sliced cremini mushrooms

1 tablespoon sesame seeds

Handful of fresh cilantro leaves

For the dressing, mix:

1 teaspoon light soy sauce

Pinch of salt and pepper

2 tablespoons puréed silken tofu

1 teaspoon chili powder

GOAT CHEESE, PEAR, CARROT & HAZELNUTS

For the salad, assemble:

1 large carrot, shaved into ribbons with a vegetable peeler
1 pear, chopped
½ cup crumbled goat cheese
Handful of blanched hazelnuts, chopped
Handful of pomegranate seeds
Handful of fresh thyme leaves

For the dressing, mix:

1 tablespoon extra virgin olive oil
1 teaspoon balsamic vinegar
Pinch of salt and pepper

PESCATARIAN ALTERNATIVE

Add 2 ounces smoked mackerel

CELERY, RADISH, BEET & RAW HORSERADISH CREAM

For the salad, assemble:

2 celery stalks, sliced
Handful of radishes, chopped
1 small beet, grated
Handful of dried blueberries
Handful of pine nuts
Bunch of fresh chives, chopped

For the dressing, blend together:

2 ounces freshly grated horseradish
1 teaspoon cider vinegar
Pinch of salt
¼ cup water (or more if needed to facilitate blending)
2 tablespoons extra virgin olive oil

VEGAN ALTERNATIVE

Replace the trout with ½ roasted sweet potato, and replace the dressing with the one on the opposite page

QUINOA, SMOKED TROUT & BEET

For the salad, assemble:

½ cup cooked red and white quinoa
1 beet, very thinly sliced (or shaved with
  a vegetable peeler)
2 ounces smoked trout, flaked
Bunch of fresh chives, chopped

For the dressing, mix:

1 tablespoon extra virgin olive oil
1 teaspoon cider vinegar
Pinch of salt and pepper
1 teaspoon horseradish sauce

COUSCOUS, BLACK BEANS, ENDIVE & POMEGRANATE

For the salad, assemble:

Scant ⅔ cup cooked whole-wheat couscous
1 head of red Belgian endive, chopped
⅓ cup canned black beans
Handful of pomegranate seeds
Bunch of fresh chives, chopped

For the dressing, mix:

1 tablespoon extra virgin olive oil
1 teaspoon balsamic vinegar
Pinch of salt and pepper

SALMON CAVIAR, JASMINE RICE, CUCUMBER & NORI

For the salad, assemble:

½ cup cooked jasmine rice
¾ cup chopped cucumber
Handful of shredded nori (toasted seaweed)
2 scallions, sliced
2 tablespoons salmon caviar

For the dressing, mix:

1 tablespoon toasted sesame oil
1 teaspoon dark soy sauce
Pinch of salt

VEGAN

PESCATARIAN ALTERNATIVE

Add ⅓ cup canned tuna (preserved in water)

ROASTED POTATOES, BLACK OLIVES & CAPERS

For the salad, assemble:

2 ounces lettuce, such as frisée
2 roasted potatoes, chopped
4 to 6 pitted black olives, halved
2 scallions, sliced
1 tablespoon capers

For the dressing, mix:

1 tablespoon extra virgin olive oil
1 teaspoon cider vinegar
Pinch of salt and pepper

ROASTED SALMON, POTATOES, BLACK QUINOA & PARSNIP

For the salad, assemble:

1 parsnip, shaved into ribbons with
 a vegetable peeler
3½ ounces halved and roasted new potatoes
Generous ¼ cup cooked black quinoa
2 ounces roasted salmon, flaked
Handful of fresh flat-leaf parsley leaves

For the dressing, mix:

1 tablespoon extra virgin olive oil
1 teaspoon balsamic vinegar
Pinch of salt and pepper

OMNIVORE

PESCATARIAN ALTERNATIVE
Replace the ham with 2 ounces roasted salmon or smoked mackerel

HAM, ROASTED POTATOES, CARROT & DRIED CRANBERRIES

For the salad, assemble:

1 large carrot, shaved into ribbons with a vegetable peeler
1 ounce arugula
3 halved and roasted new potatoes
Handful of dried cranberries
2 ounces ham, thinly sliced
Handful of fresh flat-leaf parsley leaves

For the dressing, mix:

1 tablespoon extra virgin olive oil
1 teaspoon balsamic vinegar
Pinch of salt and pepper

VEGAN

PESCATARIAN ALTERNATIVE

Add 2 ounces canned tuna (preserved in water), sardines, or anchovies, and some parsley

ROASTED POTATOES, CHERRY TOMATOES & CHILE

For the salad, assemble:

3½ ounces halved and steamed new potatoes, tossed with olive oil and finely chopped parsley
1⅓ cups cherry tomatoes, halved
1 small red onion, thinly sliced
Handful of capers
1 small chile, thinly sliced

For the dressing, mix:

1 tablespoon extra virgin olive oil
1 teaspoon cider vinegar
Pinch of salt and pepper

VEGETARIAN
ALTERNATIVE
*Add 2 ounces blue cheese
or goat cheese*

KALE, APPLE & DRIED APRICOTS

For the salad, assemble:

Scant 1 cup chopped kale (discard the stems)
1 apple, chopped
Handful of dried apricots, chopped
Handful of pine nuts

For the dressing, mix:

1 tablespoon extra virgin olive oil
1 teaspoon cider vinegar
Pinch of salt and pepper

OMNIVORE
ALTERNATIVE
Replace the tuna with
2 ounces roast beef or
smoked ham

QUAIL EGGS, TUNA, KALE & CELERY

For the salad, assemble:

½ cup chopped kale (discard the stems)
3 celery stalks, sliced
6 hard-boiled quail eggs
2 ounces canned tuna (preserved in water), flaked
Bunch of fresh chives, chopped

For the dressing, mix:

1 tablespoon extra virgin olive oil
1 teaspoon cider vinegar
Pinch of celery salt
2 tablespoons mayonnaise

OMNIVORE

VEGAN ALTERNATIVE

Replace the turkey with ½ cup quinoa, canned white beans, or green lentils

ROASTED TURKEY, MUSHROOMS, CARROT & WALNUTS

For the salad, assemble:

2 ounces mixed salad greens (e.g., chard and spinach)

1 small carrot, shaved into ribbons with a vegetable peeler

Handful of (fresh or roasted) cremini mushrooms, sliced

2 ounces roasted turkey, sliced

Handful of walnuts

Bunch of fresh chives, chopped

For the dressing, mix:

1 tablespoon extra virgin olive oil

1 teaspoon cider vinegar

Pinch of salt and pepper

ROASTED SWEET POTATO, BROCCOLI & CARROT

For the salad, assemble:

½ roasted sweet potato, chopped
1 large carrot, shaved into ribbons with a
  vegetable peeler
3½ ounces raw or steamed broccoli,
  chopped
2 scallions, sliced
Handful of fresh flat-leaf parsley leaves
Handful of pine nuts

For the dressing, mix:

1 tablespoon extra virgin olive oil
1 teaspoon cider vinegar
Pinch of salt and pepper

VEGAN

VEGETARIAN ALTERNATIVE
Add scant ¼ cup cheese, such as ricotta or cottage cheese

ROASTED SWEET POTATO, BLACK LENTILS & PISTACHIOS

For the salad, assemble:

2 ounces mixed baby salad greens (e.g., chard, watercress, and red oakleaf lettuce)
⅓ cup canned black (or green) lentils
½ roasted sweet potato, cut into wedges
2 scallions, sliced
Handful of pistachios

For the dressing, mix:

1 tablespoon extra virgin olive oil
1 teaspoon balsamic vinegar
Pinch of salt and pepper

BLACK RICE, ROASTED SWEET POTATO & PECORINO

For the salad, assemble:

½ cup cooked black rice
Handful of roasted tomatoes stored in oil
½ roasted sweet potato, chopped
1 cup pecorino shavings
Handful of pine nuts
Handful of fresh basil leaves

For the dressing, mix:

1 tablespoon extra virgin olive oil
1 teaspoon balsamic vinegar
Pinch of salt and pepper

VEGETARIAN ALTERNATIVE

Omit the water and cashews from the dressing; replace with plain yogurt

FENNEL, APPLE, CELERY & CASHEW CREAM

For the salad, assemble:

½ fennel bulb, thinly sliced
½ apple, cut into wedges
1 celery stalk, sliced
Handful of pomegranate seeds
Handful of raisins
Handful of pumpkin seeds
Sprinkle of fresh thyme leaves

For the dressing, blend together:

1 tablespoon extra virgin olive oil
1 teaspoon cider vinegar
Pinch of salt
1 tablespoon water
Handful of cashews

RAW
ALTERNATIVE
Replace the blue cheese
with Nut & Lemon
dressing (page 26, made
with walnuts)

BLUE CHEESE, APPLE, CAULIFLOWER & WALNUTS

For the salad, assemble:

1 apple, chopped
3½ ounces cauliflower, chopped
Generous ¼ cup chopped blue cheese
Handful of walnuts
Bunch of fresh chives, chopped

For the dressing, mix:

1 tablespoon extra virgin olive oil
1 teaspoon cider vinegar
Pinch of salt and pepper

BARLEY, ROASTED SWEET POTATO & EDAMAME

For the salad, assemble:

Scant ⅔ cup cooked barley
½ cup shredded kale (discard the stems)
½ roasted sweet potato, chopped
2 ounces steamed edamame
Bunch of fresh chives, chopped

For the dressing, mix:

1 tablespoon extra virgin olive oil
1 teaspoon balsamic vinegar
Pinch of salt and pepper

OMNIVORE

VEGAN
ALTERNATIVE
*Replace the chicken with
²⁄₃ cup canned cannellini
or lima beans*

ROASTED SWEET POTATO, CHICKEN & BROWN RICE

For the salad, assemble:

½ cup cooked brown short-grain rice
⅓ cup shredded green or savoy cabbage
½ roasted sweet potato, chopped
2 ounces roasted chicken, sliced
Handful of almonds, chopped
Bunch of fresh chives, chopped

For the dressing, mix:

1 tablespoon extra virgin olive oil
1 teaspoon cider vinegar
Pinch of salt and pepper
1 tablespoon Dijon whole-grain mustard

PROSCIUTTO, PEAR & PINE NUTS

For the salad, assemble:

*2 ounces mixed salad greens (e.g., watercress, arugula,
  and red oakleaf lettuce)*
1 pear, chopped
2 ounces prosciutto, thinly sliced
Handful of pine nuts

For the dressing, mix:

1 tablespoon extra virgin olive oil
1 teaspoon balsamic vinegar
Pinch of salt and pepper

VEGETARIAN ALTERNATIVE

Add 2 ounces blue cheese, such as Stilton or Gorgonzola piccante

PEAR, DATES, CASHEWS & ENDIVE

For the salad, assemble:

1 head of Belgian endive
1 large pear, chopped
Handful of dried, pitted dates, halved
Handful of cashews
Bunch of fresh chives, chopped

For the dressing, mix:

1 tablespoon extra virgin olive oil
1 teaspoon lemon juice
Pinch of salt and pepper

CANNELLINI BEANS, PECORINO, PINE NUTS & WATERCRESS

For the salad, assemble:

2 ounces watercress
⅔ cup canned cannellini beans
Handful of fresh basil leaves
Handful of pine nuts
1 cup pecorino shavings

For the dressing, mix:

1 tablespoon extra virgin olive oil
1 teaspoon balsamic vinegar
Pinch of salt and pepper
2 tablespoons Classic Pesto (page 25)

NEW POTATOES, PEAS & RED LETTUCE

For the salad, assemble:

2 ounces baby red lettuce
3½ ounces halved and steamed new potatoes
Scant ⅔ cup steamed peas
Handful of fresh flat-leaf parsley leaves

For the dressing, blend together:

1 teaspoon extra virgin olive oil
1 teaspoon cider vinegar
1 tablespoon vegan cream (e.g., soy or coconut)
Pinch of salt and pepper
1 tablespoon capers

TUNA, COUSCOUS, KALE, GREEN LENTILS & RED ONION

For the salad, assemble:

Scant ⅔ cup cooked whole-wheat couscous
⅔ cup chopped kale (discard the stems)
⅔ cup canned green lentils
2 ounces canned tuna (preserved in water), flaked
1 sliced and roasted red onion

For the dressing, mix:

1 tablespoon extra virgin olive oil
1 teaspoon lemon juice
Pinch of salt and pepper

PASTRAMI, CORNICHONS & CROUTONS

For the salad, assemble:

2½ ounces mixed salad greens (e.g., wild arugula)
Handful of cornichons (cocktail pickles)
2 ounces pastrami, thinly sliced
Handful of whole-wheat croutons

For the dressing, mix:

1 tablespoon extra virgin olive oil
1 teaspoon cider vinegar
Pinch of salt and pepper
1 teaspoon English mustard
1 tablespoon light cream

ANCHOVIES, CRANBERRY BEANS & ARUGULA

For the salad, assemble:

2 ounces arugula
2/3 cup canned cranberry beans
2 ounces marinated anchovies
Handful of pine nuts
Handful of fresh flat-leaf parsley leaves

For the dressing, mix:

1 tablespoon extra virgin olive oil
1 teaspoon cider vinegar
Pinch of salt and pepper

RASPBERRIES, RED CABBAGE & FENNEL

For the salad, assemble:

Scant 1 cup shredded red cabbage
1 small fennel bulb, thinly sliced
Handful of raspberries
Handful of pumpkin seeds
Handful of fresh mint leaves

For the dressing, mix:

1 tablespoon extra virgin olive oil
1 teaspoon lemon juice
Pinch of salt and pepper

SASHIMI TUNA, PINK GRAPEFRUIT & CHILE

For the salad, assemble:

2 ounces arugula
2 ounces sashimi tuna, very thinly sliced
½ big pink grapefruit, chopped
1 small red onion, finely chopped
1 small red chile, seeded and finely chopped
1 tablespoon toasted sesame seeds

For the dressing, mix:

1 tablespoon extra virgin olive oil
1 teaspoon lemon juice
Pinch of salt and pepper

RAW

PESCATARIAN ALTERNATIVE

Add 2 ounces cooked shrimp or smoked mackerel

PINK GRAPEFRUIT, AVOCADO & CABBAGE

For the salad, assemble:

Scant 1 cup shredded green cabbage
1 ripe avocado, chopped
½ large pink grapefruit, chopped
Handful of pine nuts
Handful of pomegranate seeds

For the dressing, mix:

1 tablespoon extra virgin olive oil
1 teaspoon lemon juice
Pinch of salt and pepper

OMNIVORE
ALTERNATIVE
*Add 2 ounces roasted
chicken, prosciutto, or
another cured ham*

PEAR, ORANGE, RED CABBAGE & POPPY SEEDS

For the salad, assemble:

Generous 1 cup shredded red cabbage
1 pear, chopped
1 orange, chopped
Handful of walnuts
1 tablespoon poppy seeds
Handful of fresh flat-leaf parsley leaves

For the dressing, mix:

1 tablespoon extra virgin olive oil
1 teaspoon lemon juice
Pinch of salt and pepper

RAW ALTERNATIVE
Replace the beef with a handful of walnuts, and the dressing with Raw Nut & Agave (page 27)

ROAST BEEF, CAULIFLOWER & RED CABBAGE

For the salad, assemble:

⅔ cup shredded red cabbage

3½ ounces cauliflower, chopped

2 ounces roast beef, thinly sliced

Handful of dried cranberries

Handful of pine nuts

Handful of fresh flat-leaf parsley leaves

For the dressing, mix:

2 tablespoons extra virgin olive oil

1 teaspoon cider vinegar

Pinch of salt and pepper

1 teaspoon light cream

1 teaspoon Dijon mustard

OMNIVORE

VEGAN ALTERNATIVE
Replace the ham with smoked tofu

PROSCIUTTO, ENOKI MUSHROOMS & ASPARAGUS

For the salad, assemble:

1 small parsnip, shaved into ribbons with a vegetable peeler

3 asparagus spears, shaved into ribbons with a vegetable peeler

2 ounces purple broccolini, chopped

Handful of enoki mushrooms

2 ounces prosciutto, thinly sliced

Handful of toasted hazelnuts, chopped

Handful of fresh basil leaves

For the dressing, mix:

1 tablespoon extra virgin olive oil

1 teaspoon balsamic vinegar

Pinch of salt and pepper

VEGETARIAN ALTERNATIVE

Replace the water with light cream or plain yogurt

PARSNIP, PINK GRAPEFRUIT & POPPY SEEDS

For the salad, assemble:

1 parsnip, shaved into ribbons with a vegetable peeler
1 pink grapefruit (or blood orange), chopped
Handful of raisins
Sprinkle of poppy seeds
Handful of fresh mint leaves

For the dressing, blend together:

1 teaspoon lemon juice
2 tablespoons unsweetened shredded coconut
2 tablespoons water
Pinch of salt
¾-inch fresh ginger, peeled and grated

CAULIFLOWER, GREEN BEANS & SPINACH

For the salad, assemble:

2 ounces baby spinach
3½ ounces cauliflower, chopped
3½ ounces steamed green beans
Handful of pine nuts
1 cup pecorino shavings
Handful of fresh basil leaves

For the dressing, mix:

1 tablespoon extra virgin olive oil
1 teaspoon balsamic vinegar
2 tablespoons Classic Pesto (page 25)
Pinch of salt and pepper

SMOKED MACKEREL, KALE & MARINATED PEPPERS

For the salad, assemble:

*½ cup chopped and steamed kale (or raw and
   massaged with lemon juice and left for 5 minutes)*
Handful of marinated red peppers from a jar, chopped
2 ounces smoked mackerel, flaked
Handful of crispy onions
Handful of fresh flat-leaf parsley leaves

For the dressing, mix:

1 tablespoon extra virgin olive oil
1 teaspoon lemon juice
Pinch of salt and pepper

OMNIVORE
ALTERNATIVE
*Add 3 1/2 ounces roasted
chicken or beef*

CARROT, RED ONION, WALNUTS & RAISINS

For the salad, assemble:

2 ounces mâche
*1 carrot, shaved into ribbons with
   a vegetable peeler*
1/2 small red onion, thinly sliced
Handful of raisins
Handful of walnuts, chopped

For the dressing, mix:

1 tablespoon extra virgin olive oil
1 teaspoon cider vinegar
Pinch of salt and pepper
1 tablespoon mustard seeds, soaked overnight

VEGAN

VEGETARIAN ALTERNATIVE
Add 2 ounces cheese, such as goat cheese, Manchego, or blue cheese

QUINOA, ROASTED SWEET POTATO & CAULIFLOWER

For the salad, assemble:

½ cup cooked red and white quinoa
2 ounces radicchio, shredded
½ roasted sweet potato, chopped
3½ ounces cauliflower, chopped
Handful of fresh flat-leaf parsley leaves

For the dressing, mix:

1 tablespoon extra virgin olive oil
1 teaspoon cider vinegar
Pinch of salt
Pinch of crushed fennel seeds

VEGETARIAN ALTERNATIVE

Add 2 ounces feta, Parmesan, or pecorino

ROASTED POTATOES & SUN-DRIED TOMATOES

For the salad, assemble:

2½ ounces mixed baby salad greens (e.g., watercress, chard, and red oakleaf lettuce)

2 roasted potatoes, chopped

Handful of sun-dried tomatoes, chopped

2 scallions, sliced

For the dressing, mix:

1 tablespoon extra virgin olive oil

1 teaspoon cider vinegar

Pinch of salt and pepper

Pinch of dried red pepper flakes

ROAST BEEF, CABBAGE & MARINATED PEPPERS

For the salad, assemble:

Generous 1 cup shredded white cabbage
¼ red onion, finely chopped
2 ounces marinated peppers from a jar, chopped
Handful of pitted kalamata olives
2 ounces roast beef, thinly sliced
Sprinkle of garlic sprouts
Handful of pine nuts

For the dressing, mix:

1 tablespoon extra virgin olive oil
1 teaspoon balsamic vinegar
Pinch of salt and pepper

SHRIMP, AVOCADO & RED RICE

For the salad, assemble:

½ cup cooked red rice
1 ounce arugula
1 avocado, chopped
2 ounces cooked shrimp
2 scallions, sliced
Sprinkle of sesame seeds

For the dressing, mix:

1 tablespoon extra virgin olive oil
Pinch of salt
1 tablespoon mayonnaise
Pinch of saffron powder
Pinch of ground turmeric

MANGO, SNOW PEAS, BOK CHOY & BROCCOLI

For the salad, assemble:

¾ cup finely chopped bok choy or spring greens
Handful of snow peas or sugar snap peas
3½ ounces broccoli, chopped
3½ ounces mango, cubed
2 scallions, sliced
Handful of fresh basil leaves

For the dressing, mix:

1 tablespoon extra virgin olive oil
1 teaspoon cider vinegar
Pinch of salt
Pinch of dried red pepper flakes

OMNIVORE

VEGETARIAN ALTERNATIVE
Replace the roast beef with 2 ounces Gouda cheese, Manchego, or Ossau-Iraty

ROAST BEEF, BLACK LENTILS & MUSHROOMS

For the salad, assemble:

2¼ ounces watercress
⅔ cup canned black lentils
Handful of cremini mushrooms, sliced
2 ounces roast beef, thinly sliced
Bunch of fresh chives, chopped

For the dressing, mix:

1 tablespoon extra virgin olive oil
1 tablespoon truffle-infused olive oil
1 teaspoon balsamic vinegar
Pinch of salt and pepper

VEGETARIAN

VEGAN ALTERNATIVE

Replace the egg and cheese with ½ roasted sweet potato or 3½ ounces roasted butternut squash

QUINOA, EGG, MANCHEGO, BLACK OLIVES & PICKLES

For the salad, assemble:

½ cup cooked red and white quinoa
1 hard-boiled egg, chopped
Small handful of pitted black olives, halved
Generous ¼ cup chopped Manchego, Cheddar cheese,
  or other mild cheese
4 to 6 cornichons (cocktail pickles)
4 to 6 baby pickled onions
Handful of fresh flat-leaf parsley leaves

For the dressing, mix:

1 tablespoon extra virgin olive oil
1 teaspoon balsamic vinegar
Pinch of salt and pepper

CHEDDAR, BLACK BEANS & SUN-DRIED TOMATOES

For the salad, assemble:

²/₃ *cup shredded white cabbage*
²/₃ *cup canned black beans*
¹/₂ *small red onion, finely chopped*
Handful of sun-dried tomatoes, chopped
Generous ¹/₄ cup cubed sharp Cheddar cheese
Handful of fresh cilantro leaves

For the dressing, mix:

1 tablespoon extra virgin olive oil
1 teaspoon cider vinegar
Pinch of salt
Pinch of dried red pepper flakes

OMNIVORE
ALTERNATIVE
*Add 2 ounces roasted
chicken, beef, or ham*

PARSNIP, ASPARAGUS, PINE NUTS & RAW PESTO

For the salad, assemble:

*3 asparagus spears, shaved into ribbons with
  a vegetable peeler*
*1 parsnip (or carrot), shaved into ribbons with
  a vegetable peeler*
Handful of pine nuts
Handful of fresh flat-leaf parsley leaves

For the dressing, mix:

1 tablespoon extra virgin olive oil
1 teaspoon cider vinegar
Pinch of salt and pepper
2 tablespoons Raw Green Pesto (page 25)

VEGETARIAN

PESCATARIAN ALTERNATIVE

Replace the cottage cheese with 2 ounces smoked mackerel or salmon

ROASTED SWEET POTATO, QUINOA & COTTAGE CHEESE

For the salad, assemble:

¹/₂ cup shredded spring greens
¹/₂ cup cooked red quinoa
¹/₂ roasted sweet potato, chopped
2 tablespoons cottage cheese
Handful of fresh flat-leaf parsley leaves

For the dressing, mix:

1 tablespoon extra virgin olive oil
1 teaspoon cider vinegar
Pinch of salt and pepper

VEGAN

VEGETARIAN ALTERNATIVE
Add 2 ounces goat cheese, blue cheese, or pecorino

ROASTED SWEET POTATO, LIMA BEANS & PISTACHIOS

For the salad, assemble:

2 ounces pea shoots or watercress
²/₃ cup canned lima or fava beans
¹/₂ roasted sweet potato, chopped
Handful of pistachios

For the dressing, mix:

1 tablespoon extra virgin olive oil
1 teaspoon cider vinegar
Pinch of salt and pepper

CAULIFLOWER, AVOCADO & GOJI BERRIES

For the salad, assemble:

2 ounces mâche
2 ounces cauliflower, chopped
1 avocado, chopped
Handful of dried goji berries
Handful of pine nuts

For the dressing, mix:

1 tablespoon extra virgin olive oil
1 teaspoon cider vinegar
Pinch of salt and pepper
Pinch of saffron threads
2 tablespoons Raw Nut & Agave dressing
  (page 27, made with pine nuts)

SHRIMP, MANGO, SCALLIONS & CHILI

For the salad, assemble:

2½ ounces mixed salad greens
½ small mango, cubed
Handful of cooked shrimp
2 scallions, sliced
Handful of fresh cilantro leaves

For the dressing, mix:

1 tablespoon sunflower oil
1 teaspoon light soy sauce (or Thai fish sauce)
Pinch of salt and pepper
Pinch of dried red pepper flakes

BROWN RICE, MOZZARELLA & MUSHROOMS

For the salad, assemble:

½ cup cooked brown short-grain rice
Scant 1½ cups chopped and roasted cremini mushrooms
Generous ¼ cup chopped mozzarella
Handful of fresh basil leaves

For the dressing, mix:

1 tablespoon extra virgin olive oil
1 teaspoon cider vinegar
Pinch of salt and pepper

ROASTED CHICKEN, QUINOA, FAVA BEANS & CORN

For the salad, assemble:

½ cup cooked red and white quinoa
1 small avocado, chopped
Generous ¼ cup fresh or canned corn
2 ounces steamed fava beans
2 ounces roasted chicken, chopped
Handful of fresh cilantro leaves

For the dressing, mix:

1 tablespoon extra virgin olive oil
2 tablespoons coconut cream or puréed silken tofu
¾–inch fresh ginger, peeled and grated
Pinch of salt and pepper

OMNIVORE ALTERNATIVE

Replace mackerel with 2 ounces roast beef or ham; add 1 teaspoon mustard to the dressing

SMOKED MACKEREL, ROASTED POTATOES & KALE

For the salad, assemble:

½ cup chopped kale (discard the stems)
3 roasted new potatoes, chopped
Handful of dried cranberries
3½ ounces smoked mackerel, flaked
2 scallions, sliced

For the dressing, mix:

1 tablespoon extra virgin olive oil
1 teaspoon lemon juce
Pinch of salt and pepper

BLACK BEANS, AVOCADO, SHALLOT & CHILE

For the salad, assemble:

2 ounces mâche
⅔ cup canned black beans
1 avocado, chopped
1 small shallot, thinly sliced
1 small red chile, seeded and minced
Handful of fresh flat-leaf parsley leaves

For the dressing, mix:

1 tablespoon extra virgin olive oil
1 teaspoon lemon juce
Pinch of salt and pepper

VEGAN

OMNIVORE
ALTERNATIVE
*Add 2 ounces roasted
chicken*

COUSCOUS, BLACK LENTILS & PISTACHIOS

For the salad, assemble:

*Scant ⅔ cup couscous cooked with a pinch of dried
 parsley and coriander*
⅔ cup canned black lentils
Handful of pistachios
Handful of fresh cilantro leaves

For the dressing, mix:

1 tablespoon extra virgin olive oil
1 teaspoon cider vinegar
Pinch of salt and pepper
2 tablespoons lemon and cilantro hummus

PINK GRAPEFUIT, BROCCOLI, KALE & CAPERS

For the salad, assemble:

½ cup chopped kale (discard the stems)
3½ ounces purple broccolini, chopped
1 pink grapefruit, chopped
1 tablespoon capers
Handful of almonds, chopped

For the dressing, mix:

1 tablespoon extra virgin olive oil
1 teaspoon lemon juice
Pinch of salt and pepper

VEGETARIAN
ALTERNATIVE
*Replace the Nut &
Lemon dressing
with plain yogurt or
heavy cream*

CARROT, ORANGE, DRIED APRICOTS & PISTACHIOS

For the salad, assemble:

*2 small carrots, shredded with a
    julienne peeler*
1 orange, chopped
*Handful of dried apricots,
    chopped*
Handful of pistachios
*Sprinkle of lemon zest, removed with
    a vegetable peeler*

For the dressing, mix:

1 tablespoon extra virgin olive oil
1 teaspoon lemon juice
Pinch of salt and pepper
*2 tablespoons Nut & Lemon dressing (page 26,
    made with cashews)*

OMNIVORE ALTERNATIVE

Replace the smoked mackerel with smoked ham

SMOKED MACKEREL, PURPLE CARROT & AVOCADO

For the salad, assemble:

1 purple (or regular) carrot, shaved into ribbons with
  a vegetable peeler
½ avocado, chopped
Handful of roasted tomatoes stored in oil
2 ounces smoked mackerel, flaked
Handful of pine nuts
1 tablespoon poppy seeds
Handful of fresh lemon thyme leaves

For the dressing, mix:

1 tablespoon extra virgin olive oil
1 teaspoon balsamic vinegar
Pinch of salt and pepper

VEGAN

OMNIVORE ALTERNATIVE

Add 2 ounces roasted chicken or chorizo

QUINOA, SUN-DRIED TOMATOES, PARSNIP & CRISPY ONIONS

For the salad, assemble:

1 large parsnip, shaved into ribbons with a vegetable peeler

½ cup cooked red and white quinoa

1 tablespoon crispy onions

2 ounces sun-dried tomatoes

Handful of fresh basil leaves

For the dressing, mix:

1 tablespoon extra virgin olive oil

1 teaspoon balsamic vinegar

Pinch of salt and pepper

VEGAN ALTERNATIVE

Replace the salmon with ⅔ cup canned kidney, borlotti, or adzuki beans

ROASTED SALMON, QUINOA, PARSNIP & KALE

For the salad, assemble:

⅔ cup shredded kale (discard the stems)

Generous ¼ cup cooked black quinoa

1 small parsnip, shaved into ribbons with a vegetable peeler

2 ounces marinated red peppers from a jar, chopped

5 ounces roasted salmon, flaked

Handful of fresh flat-leaf parsley leaves

For the dressing, mix:

1 tablespoon extra virgin olive oil

1 teaspoon balsamic vinegar

Pinch of salt and pepper

VEGETARIAN

VEGAN ALTERNATIVE
Replace the blue cheese with ⅔ cup canned green or black lentils

CAULIFLOWER, BLUE CHEESE & MARINATED PEPPERS

For the salad, assemble:

1 ounce arugula
3½ ounces cauliflower, chopped
Handful of marinated red and yellow peppers from a jar
½ cup crumbled blue cheese
Handful of pumpkin seeds
Bunch of fresh chives, chopped

For the dressing, mix:

1 tablespoon extra virgin olive oil
1 teaspoon balsamic vinegar
Pinch of salt and pepper

RAW
ALTERNATIVE
*Replace the roasted
salmon and artichokes
with cherry tomatoes
and pecans*

ROASTED SALMON, CAULIFLOWER & ARTICHOKES

For the salad, assemble:

3¹/₂ ounces cauliflower, finely chopped

*Handful of grilled, marinated artichoke hearts,
  chopped*

2 ounces roasted salmon, flaked

2 scallions, sliced

1 tablespoon poppy seeds

Handful of fresh cilantro leaves

For the dressing, mix:

1 tablespoon extra virgin olive oil

1 teaspoon lemon juice

Pinch of salt and pepper

RAW

VEGAN ALTERNATIVE
Add ⅔ cup canned lima beans or black-eyed peas

SUN-DRIED TOMATOES, AVOCADO & RADICCHIO

For the salad, assemble:

2 ounces radicchio
1 avocado, chopped
2 ounces sun-dried tomatoes
Handful of pine nuts
1 small shallot, thinly sliced
Handful of fresh flat-leaf parsley leaves

For the dressing, mix:

1 tablespoon extra virgin olive oil
1 teaspoon lemon juice
Pinch of salt and pepper

VEGAN

OMNIVORE
ALTERNATIVE
*Add 2 ounces chorizo,
ham, or roast beef*

CHICKPEAS, BLACK OLIVES & SUN-DRIED TOMATOES

For the salad, assemble:

2 ounces red oakleaf lettuce
⅔ cup canned chickpeas
2 ounces sun-dried tomatoes
Handful of pitted black olives, halved
1 tablespoon toasted sesame seeds
Handful of fresh flat-leaf parsley leaves

For the dressing, mix:

1 tablespoon extra virgin olive oil
1 teaspoon lemon juice
Pinch of salt and pepper
2 tablespoons hummus

BROILED SQUID, AVOCADO, EDAMAME & CHILE

For the salad, assemble:

2 ounces arugula
1 avocado, chopped
2 ounces steamed edamame
2 ounces broiled squid, sliced
1 small red chile, seeded and chopped
Handful of fresh cilantro leaves

For the dressing, mix:

1 tablespoon extra virgin olive oil
1 teaspoon lemon juice
Pinch of salt and pepper
¾–inch fresh ginger, peeled and grated

RAW
ALTERNATIVE
Replace the chicken
with cashews, and the
coconut cream with Raw
Nut & Agave
(page 27)

ROASTED CHICKEN, YELLOW CARROT & PURPLE BROCCOLI

For the salad, assemble:

½ cup chopped spring greens
1 small yellow (or regular) carrot, shaved into ribbons
   with a vegetable peeler
½ avocado, chopped
2 ounces purple broccolini, chopped
2 ounces roasted chicken, sliced
Handful of fresh flat-leaf parsley leaves

For the dressing, mix:

1 tablespoon extra virgin olive oil
2 tablespoons coconut cream or puréed silken tofu
¾-inch fresh ginger, peeled and grated
Pinch of salt and pepper

OMNIVORE
ALTERNATIVE
*Add some pan-fried
pancetta cubes or chorizo*

PASTA, GREEN BEANS, KALE & COTTAGE CHEESE

For the salad, assemble:

3¹⁄₂ ounces cooked whole-wheat fusilli
Scant ¹⁄₂ cup chopped kale (discard the stems)
Handful of steamed green beans
Handful of sun-dried tomatoes
Scant ¹⁄₄ cup cottage cheese
Handful of fresh basil leaves

For the dressing, mix:

1 tablespoon extra virgin olive oil
1 teaspoon balsamic vinegar
Pinch of salt and pepper

VEGAN

PESCATARIAN
ALTERNATIVE
*Add 2 ounces cooked
shrimp*

WILD RICE, CAULIFLOWER & SPRING GREENS

For the salad, assemble:

½ cup cooked wild rice
⅓ cup finely chopped spring greens
3½ ounces cauliflower, chopped
Bunch of fresh chives, chopped

For the dressing, blend together:

1 tablespoon sun-dried tomatoes
1 tablespoon extra virgin olive oil
1 teaspoon cider vinegar
Pinch of salt and pepper
Pinch of dried red pepper flakes
1 teaspoon water

RED CABBAGE, BLACK LENTILS & CARROT

For the salad, assemble:

⅔ cup canned black lentils
Generous 1 cup shredded red cabbage
1 carrot, shaved into ribbons with a vegetable peeler
Handful of pine nuts
Bunch of fresh chives, chopped

For the dressing, blend together:

1 tablespoon sun-dried tomatoes
1 tablespoon extra virgin olive oil
1 teaspoon cider vinegar
Pinch of salt and pepper
1 teaspoon water

VEGAN ALTERNATIVE

Replace the goat cheese with 3 ½ ounces tomatoes or ½ roasted sweet potato

GOAT CHEESE, BROWN LENTILS & PINE NUTS

For the salad, assemble:

2 ounces mixed salad greens (e.g., frisée, mâche, and radicchio)
⅔ cup canned brown lentils
Generous ¼ cup chopped firm goat cheese or Brie
Handful of pine nuts
Bunch of fresh chives, chopped

For the dressing, mix:

1 tablespoon extra virgin olive oil
1 teaspoon cider vinegar
Pinch of salt and pepper
Pinch of ground cumin

ROASTED CHICKEN, BROWN RICE & BLACK BEANS

For the salad, assemble:

½ cup cooked brown short-grain rice

⅔ cup canned black beans

2 ounces marinated red peppers from a jar, chopped

2 ounces roasted chicken, sliced

Handful of pumpkin seeds

Handful of fresh mint leaves

For the dressing, mix:

1 tablespoon extra virgin olive oil

1 teaspoon balsamic vinegar

Pinch of salt and pepper

Pinch of smoked paprika

VEGETARIAN ALTERNATIVE

Replace the salmon with 2 hard-boiled eggs

SASHIMI SALMON, AVOCADO & JASMINE RICE

For the salad, assemble:

½ cup cooked jasmine rice
Handful of baby watercress
1 avocado, chopped
2 ounces sashimi salmon, thinly sliced
Bunch of fresh chives, chopped

For the dressing, mix:

2 tablespoons toasted sesame (or sunflower) oil
2 teaspoons dark soy sauce
1 teaspoon wasabi powder

VEGAN

VEGETARIAN ALTERNATIVE
Add scant ¼ cup cottage cheese or blue cheese

ROASTED BUTTERNUT SQUASH, BLACK LENTILS & CABBAGE

For the salad, assemble:

Generous 1 cup shredded white cabbage
Scant ½ cup chopped and roasted butternut squash
⅔ cup canned black lentils
1 tablespoon sesame seeds
1 teaspoon fresh thyme leaves

For the dressing, mix:

1 tablespoon extra virgin olive oil
1 teaspoon cider vinegar
Pinch of salt and pepper

PASTA, MOZZARELLA, CAPERS & SUN-DRIED TOMATOES

For the salad, assemble:

3¹/₂ ounces cooked whole-wheat fusilli
Handful of sun-dried tomatoes, chopped
Handful of capers
2 ounces mini mozzarella balls
Bunch of fresh chives, chopped

For the dressing, mix:

1 tablespoon extra virgin olive oil
1 teaspoon balsamic vinegar
Pinch of salt and pepper

OMNIVORE

VEGAN ALTERNATIVE
Replace the chorizo with ½ roasted sweet potato

CHORIZO, CROUTONS & MARINATED PEPPERS

For the salad, assemble:

2 ounces baby spinach
2 ounces marinated red peppers from a jar, chopped
2 ounces chorizo, chopped
Handful of whole-wheat croutons
1 cup pecorino shavings
Handful of fresh flat-leaf parsley leaves

For the dressing, mix:

1 tablespoon extra virgin olive oil
1 teaspoon cider vinegar
Pinch of salt and pepper

TUNA, CARROT, RED PEPPER & CROUTONS

For the salad, assemble:

Handful of arugula
1 carrot, shredded with a julienne peeler
½ red bell pepper, sliced
2 ounces canned tuna (preserved in water), flaked
Handful of whole-wheat croutons
2 scallions, sliced
Handful of fresh cilantro leaves

For the dressing, mix:

2 tablespoons mayonnaise
1 teaspoon dark soy sauce
¾–inch fresh ginger, peeled and grated

VEGETARIAN ALTERNATIVE

Add 2 ounces goat cheese and replace the Nut & Lemon dressing with heavy cream

PARSNIP, MUSHROOMS, WALNUTS & TRUFFLE CREAM

For the salad, assemble:

1 parsnip, shaved into ribbons with a vegetable peeler
Scant 1½ cups sliced cremini mushrooms
Handful of walnuts, chopped
Handful of fresh flat-leaf parsley leaves

For the dressing, mix:

1 tablespoon truffle-infused olive oil
1 teaspoon balsamic vinegar
Pinch of salt and pepper
2 tablespoons Nut & Lemon dressing
 (page 26, made with walnuts)

RED CABBAGE, CARROT, PARSNIP & EGG MAYO

For the salad, assemble:

Generous 1 cup shredded red cabbage

½ carrot, shredded with a julienne peeler

½ parsnip, shredded with a julienne peeler

1 teaspoon poppy seeds

For the dressing, mix:

1 tablespoon extra virgin olive oil

1 teaspoon cider vinegar

Pinch of salt and pepper

2 tablespoons mayonnaise

1 hard-boiled egg, finely chopped

ROASTED CHICKEN, AVOCADO & CROUTONS

For the salad, assemble:

2 ounces mixed arugula and mâche
½ avocado, chopped
2 ounces roasted chicken or turkey, sliced
Handful of whole-wheat croutons
2 scallions, sliced
1 cup Parmesan cheese shavings

For the dressing, mix:

1 tablespoon extra virgin olive oil
1 teaspoon balsamic vinegar
Pinch of salt and pepper

MOZZARELLA, ASPARAGUS & KALE

For the salad, assemble:

¾ cup chopped kale (discard the stems)
*2 asparagus spears, shaved into ribbons with
   a vegetable peeler*
Generous ¼ cup cubed mozzarella
Handful of pine nuts
Handful of fresh basil leaves

For the dressing, mix:

1 tablespoon extra virgin olive oil
1 teaspoon balsamic vinegar
Pinch of salt and pepper
2 tablespoons Classic Pesto (page 25)

VEGAN

VEGETARIAN ALTERNATIVE

Add scant ¼ cup cottage or goat cheese

CAULIFLOWER, DRIED CRANBERRIES & KALE

For the salad, assemble:

½ cup chopped kale (discard the stems)
3½ ounces cauliflower, chopped
½ small red onion, thinly sliced
Handful of pistachios
Handful of dried cranberries
Handful of whole-wheat croutons
Handful of fresh flat-leaf parsley leaves

For the dressing, mix:

1 tablespoon extra virgin olive oil
1 teaspoon balsamic vinegar
Pinch of salt and pepper

RAW

OMNIVORE
ALTERNATIVE
*Add 2 ounces roasted
chicken, beef, or ham*

CAULIFLOWER, HAZELNUTS & DRIED APRICOTS

For the salad, assemble:

2 ounces mixed baby salad greens
3¹/₂ ounces cauliflower, chopped
*Handful of dried apricots,
    chopped*
Handful of hazelnuts, chopped
Handful of fresh flat-leaf parsley leaves

For the dressing, mix:

1 tablespoon extra virgin olive oil
1 teaspoon cider vinegar
Pinch of salt and pepper

RAW ALTERNATIVE

Replace the smoked mackerel with a handful of capers and more pine nuts

SMOKED MACKEREL, CAULIFLOWER & ASPARAGUS

For the salad, assemble:

2 ounces arugula

2 asparagus spears, shaved into ribbons with a vegetable peeler

2¼ ounces cauliflower, chopped

2 ounces smoked mackerel, flaked

Handful of pine nuts

Handful of fresh flat-leaf parsley leaves

For the dressing, blend together:

1 tablespoon extra virgin olive oil

1 teaspoon lemon juice

Pinch of salt and pepper

Handful of pumpkin seeds

1 teaspoon capers

CHORIZO, BLACK QUINOA, ASPARAGUS & EDAMAME

For the salad, assemble:

2 ounces chorizo, cubed
½ cup cooked black quinoa
3½ ounces steamed edamame
*2 asparagus spears, shaved into ribbons with
  a vegetable peeler*
Bunch of fresh chives, chopped

For the dressing, mix:

1 tablespoon extra virgin olive oil
1 teaspoon balsamic vinegar
Pinch of salt and pepper

CHORIZO, BLACK RICE, PEAS & MARINATED PEPPERS

For the salad, assemble:

½ cup cooked black rice
Scant ⅔ cup steamed peas
Handful of marinated red peppers from a jar
2 ounces chorizo, sliced
Handful of pumpkin seeds
Handful of fresh flat-leaf parsley leaves

For the dressing, mix:

1 tablespoon extra virgin olive oil
1 teaspoon balsamic vinegar
Pinch of salt and pepper

RAW ALTERNATIVE

Replace the crabmeat with a handful of cashews and raisins; use raw not marinated peppers

CRABMEAT, AVOCADO & MARINATED PEPPERS

For the salad, assemble:

2¼ ounces arugula
1 avocado, chopped
Handful of marinated red peppers from a jar, chopped
2 ounces cooked crabmeat
Bunch of fresh chives, chopped

For the dressing, mix:

1 tablespoon extra virgin olive oil
1 teaspoon lemon juice
Pinch of salt and pepper

RAW

OMNIVORE
ALTERNATIVE
*Add 2 ounces roasted
chicken breast*

PURPLE BROCCOLI, MUSHROOMS & COCONUT FLAKES

For the salad, assemble:

⅔ cup shredded spring greens
Handful of white mushrooms, sliced
3½ ounces purple broccolini, chopped
½ small red chile, sliced
2 scallions, sliced
2 tablespoons unsweetened coconut flakes
Handful of fresh cilantro leaves

For the dressing, mix:

1 tablespoon extra virgin olive oil
1 teaspoon cider vinegar
Pinch of salt and pepper

VEGETARIAN
ALTERNATIVE

*Replace the anchovies
with purple broccolini*

ANCHOVIES, QUAIL EGGS, QUINOA & ASPARAGUS

For the salad, assemble:

½ cup spring greens, shredded

Generous ¼ cup cooked white and red quinoa

*1 asparagus spear, shaved into ribbons with
  a vegetable peeler*

3 to 4 hard-boiled quail eggs, halved

2 ounces marinated anchovies

Bunch of fresh chives, chopped

For the dressing, mix:

1 tablespoon extra virgin olive oil

1 teaspoon cider vinegar

Pinch of salt and pepper

OMNIVORE

VEGETARIAN ALTERNATIVE

Replace the roasted turkey with 2 ounces goat cheese

ROASTED TURKEY, BUTTERNUT SQUASH & CHICKPEAS

For the salad, assemble:

Scant 1 cup chopped kale (discard the stems)
3½ ounces roasted butternut squash, chopped
⅓ cup canned chickpeas
2 ounces roasted turkey, thinly sliced
Handful of toasted pistachios
Handful of dried cranberries
Handful of fresh flat-leaf parsley leaves

For the dressing, mix:

1 tablespoon extra virgin olive oil
1 teaspoon balsamic vinegar
Pinch of salt and pepper

EGG, ASPARAGUS, CROUTONS & PECORINO

For the salad, assemble:

2 ounces mixed baby salad greens

2 asparagus spears, shaved into ribbons with
  a vegetable peeler

1 hard-boiled egg, cut into wedges

Handful of whole-wheat croutons

Scant ¼ cup chopped pecorino

For the dressing, mix:

1 tablespoon extra virgin olive oil

1 teaspoon balsamic vinegar

Pinch of salt and pepper

RAW

VEGAN ALTERNATIVE

Replace the sprouted beans with ⅔ cup canned adzuki beans or black-eyed peas

ENOKI MUSHROOMS, AVOCADO & SPROUTED BEANS

For the salad, assemble:

Handful of mixed baby salad greens (e.g., chard, watercress, and red oakleaf lettuce)

1 avocado, chopped

2 ounces enoki mushrooms

Handful of sprouted beans (or lentils)

For the dressing, mix:

1 tablespoon extra virgin olive oil

1 teaspoon cider vinegar

Pinch of salt and pepper

OMNIVORE

VEGETARIAN ALTERNATIVE

Replace the chicken with 2 ounces Parmesan

ROASTED CHICKEN, CANNELLINI BEANS & PEA SHOOTS

For the salad, assemble:

2 ounces pea shoots or watercress
⅔ cup canned cannellini or navy beans
2 ounces roasted chicken, sliced
Handful of dried cranberries

For the dressing, mix:

1 tablespoon extra virgin olive oil
1 teaspoon cider vinegar
Pinch of salt and pepper
Pinch of saffron threads

APPLE, BROCCOLI, BOK CHOY & ALMONDS

For the salad, assemble:

⅔ cup shredded bok choy or spring greens

1 apple, chopped

3½ ounces broccoli, chopped

Handful of almonds

Handful of fresh mint leaves

For the dressing, mix:

1 tablespoon extra virgin olive oil

1 teaspoon lemon juice

Pinch of salt and pepper

2 tablespoons Nut & Lemon dressing (page 26, made with almonds)

BLACK OLIVES, CROUTONS & PARMESAN

For the salad, assemble:

3½ ounces arugula
Handful of whole-wheat croutons
⅔ cup Parmesan cheese shavings
Handful of pitted Niçoise olives
1 tablespoon toasted sesame seeds
2 scallions, sliced

For the dressing, blend together:

1 tablespoon extra virgin olive oil
1 teaspoon tahini
1 tablespoon light cream
Pinch of salt and pepper

ROAST BEEF, COUSCOUS, ASPARAGUS & KALE

For the salad, assemble:

Scant 1 cup chopped kale (discard the stems)
Scant ⅓ cup cooked couscous
*2 asparagus spears, shaved into ribbons with
   a vegetable peeler*
2 ounces roast beef, thinly sliced
Handful of fresh flat-leaf parsley leaves

For the dressing, mix:

1 tablespoon extra virgin olive oil
1 teaspoon cider vinegar
Pinch of salt and pepper
1 tablespoon Classic Pesto (page 25)

KALE, NEW POTATOES & BLACK OLIVES

For the salad, assemble:

½ cup chopped kale (discard the stems)
3½ ounces halved and steamed new
  potatoes
Handful of marinated red peppers from a jar
Handful of pitted black olives
Handful of fresh flat-leaf parsley leaves

For the dressing, mix:

1 tablespoon extra virgin olive oil
1 teaspoon cider vinegar
Pinch of salt and pepper

VEGAN

OMNIVORE ALTERNATIVE

Add 2 ounces roasted chicken or beef, or smoked ham

PINTO BEANS, ARTICHOKES & SESAME SEEDS

For the salad, assemble:

2 ounces arugula

⅔ cup canned pinto or cranberry beans

Handful of grilled, marinated artichoke hearts, chopped

1 teaspoon toasted sesame seeds

Bunch of fresh chives, chopped

For the dressing, mix:

1 tablespoon extra virgin olive oil

1 teaspoon cider vinegar

Pinch of salt and pepper

1 tablespoon artichoke purée

VEGETARIAN ALTERNATIVE
Replace the octopus with cheese, such as goat or feta

OCTOPUS, SUN-DRIED TOMATOES & NEW POTATOES

For the salad, assemble:

2 ounces arugula
3½ ounces steamed new potatoes
Handful of sun-dried tomatoes, chopped
2 ounces cooked octopus, chopped
Handful of fresh flat-leaf parsley leaves

For the dressing, mix:

1 tablespoon extra virgin olive oil
1 teaspoon balsamic vinegar
Pinch of salt and pepper

INDEX

ACKNOWLEDGMENTS

Thanks to my other half, Vera, who started this project with me because of her curiosity about nutrition. Thanks to my dad, who is always very proud and supportive even though he hates salads. Thanks to my uncle and aunty, who are always there for me. Thanks to all the people who have been there for me all these years, with affectionate support, and even those who have laughed at my crazy little project. Thanks to my colleagues at Discovery, in particular Federico, who has tested a lot of the salads, and Judy, who has always pushed me forward. Thanks to my agents for being consistently available and resourceful, even with an eight-hour time difference. Thanks to Adrian and the girls at Emerald Street, without whom this book wouldn't have happened.